Spelling

11

GRADE FIVE

ACSI Spelling

Acknowledgements

The ACSI Spelling Series is the product of a remarkable team of Christian educators.

Editorial Team

Dr. Sharon Berry—Managing Editor, Dr. Barry Morris—Content Editor,
and Dr. Ollie Gibbs—Project Director

Author Team

Mrs. Sharon Bird, Mrs. Cathy Guy, Mrs. Eunice Harris, Miss Linda Miller,
Mrs. Nancy Wetsel, and Mrs. Connie Williams

Project Consultants

Dr. Barbara Bode, Dr. Richard Edlin, Dr. Omer Bonenberger, Dr. Linda Goodson,
Dr. Alex Lackey, Mrs. Ruth McBride, Dr. Connie Pearson, Mrs. Patti Rahn,
Dr. Milton Uecker, and Dr. Ray White

To enable Christian educators and schools worldwide to effectively prepare students for life

Copyright 1991, Revised 1994, Reprinted 1999, 2001

Publishing is a function of the Academic Affairs Department of ACSI. As an organization, ACSI is committed to the ministry of Christian school education, to enable Christian educators and schools worldwide to effectively prepare students for life. As a publisher of books, textbooks, and other resources, ACSI endeavors to produce biblically sound materials that reflect Christian scholarship and stewardship, and that address the identified needs of Christian schools around the world.

For additional information, write ACSI, Academic Affairs Department, PO Box 35097, Colorado Springs, CO 80935-3509.

Printed in the United States of America

ACSI Elementary Spelling—Grade Five Student Edition
ISBN 1-58331-162-9 **Catalog # 7415**

Association of Christian Schools International
PO Box 35097 • Colorado Springs, CO • 80935-3509
Order Department: 800/367-0798 • Website: http://www.acsi.org

ACSI SPELLING

Contents • Grade Five

Page

4	*Lesson 1*	Reviewing consonants and short vowels
8	*Lesson 2*	Long vowels
12	*Lesson 3*	Vowel digraphs **ie** and **ei**
16	*Lesson 4*	Vowel digraphs
20	*Lesson 5*	At the Library
24	*Lesson 6*	Review Lessons 1-5
28	*Lesson 7*	More vowel digraphs
32	*Lesson 8*	Long **u** and **oo**
36	*Lesson 9*	Schwa **r**
40	*Lesson 10*	**R**-controlled **o**
44	*Lesson 11*	More **r**-controlled vowels
48	*Lesson 12*	Review Lessons 7-11
52	*Lesson 13*	Math Success
56	*Lesson 14*	Schwa **o**
60	*Lesson 15*	Schwa plus **l**
64	*Lesson 16*	Word Building
68	*Lesson 17*	Our World
72	*Lesson 18*	Review Lessons 13-17
76	*Lesson 19*	Words with **ti** and **si**
80	*Lesson 20*	Words with **i** or **u** after consonants
84	*Lesson 21*	Word Building
88	*Lesson 22*	Spellings and sounds of **y**
92	*Lesson 23*	Looking to the Future
96	*Lesson 24*	Review Lessons 19-23
100	*Lesson 25*	Long vowels in accented and unaccented syllables
104	*Lesson 26*	Suffixes
108	*Lesson 27*	More suffixes
112	*Lesson 28*	Word Building
116	*Lesson 29*	Visiting Court
120	*Lesson 30*	Review Lessons 25-29
124	*Lesson 31*	Homographs and homophones
128	*Lesson 32*	Consonant digraphs, clusters and silent letters
132	*Lesson 33*	Prefixes
136	*Lesson 34*	Word Building
140	*Lesson 35*	Maintaining Peace
144	*Lesson 36*	Review Lessons 31-35
148	Pronunciation Key	
149	Glossary	
168	Word Bank	
176	Personal Spelling Record	

expect
o'clock
electric
assembly
chest
suggest
whisper
attic
industry
umbrella
sandwiches
linen
cabinet
telegram
catastrophe
coconut
punished
*recently**
chilly
ridiculous

Hi, Fifth Graders! Welcome to a super year of spelling excellence.

The Word Power Team. Through the year you will be helped to gain word power by a team of friends. Their names are Captain Consonant, Victor Vowel, Wendy Word, Amy Antonym, Sam Synonym, and Roger Review. They are assisted in their duties by two robots named Pre-FixBot and Suf-FixBot. Their mission is to make learning to spell easier and more fun. Join them and enjoy them as you become a powerful speller of words this year.

A **Analogies.** Complete each of the following analogies with one of your list words.

1. Wool is to coat as _____ is to tablecloth.

2. Downstairs is to upstairs as cellar is to _____ .

3. Warm is to hot as _____ is to cold.

4. Silverware is to chest as china is to _____ .

5. Gasoline is to engine as _____ is to wire.

6. Omelets are to breakfast as _____ are to lunch.

7. Letter is to mail as message is to _____ .

8. Carrot is to vegetable as _____ is to fruit.

"I press toward the goal for the prize of the upward call of God in Christ Jesus."
(Philippians 3:14)

B **Picture This**. All of this week's words have a short vowel in them, with one exception. Match one of your spelling words to the correct shape below. A short vowel goes in each shaded box. Several of your words have two short vowels.

ă

ĕ

ĭ

ŭ

Remember that a short vowel is a schwa in unaccented syllables.

ŏ

and... no short vowel

C **Hink Pinks**. A *hink pink* is a two-word phrase that rhymes, like *hink* and *pink*. Look at the descriptions below and find a list word, plus a word that rhymes with that list word. Write the two-word phrase on the line. For example, an *unhappy boy* would be a *sad lad*.

1. The highest quality box for holding something special is the _____.

2. A cool nickname for a city in Pennsylvania is _____.

3. A crackling-fresh, soft voice is a _____.

4. A kind of electricity in the upstairs storeroom is _____.

5. To hint at putting someone in handcuffs and taking him to jail is to _____.

6. A timepiece made of stone is a _____.

7. What the person in charge does to groups of two pieces of bread with filling is _____.

5

expect
o'clock
electric
assembly
chest
suggest
whisper
attic
industry
umbrella
sandwiches
linen
cabinet
telegram
catastrophe
coconut
punished
recently
chilly
ridiculous

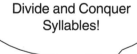

Divide and Conquer
Syllables!

D **Categorize.** Look at the pairs of words and decide how they are related. Choose one of your list words which is related in the same way.

1. meeting, gathering, _____

2. disaster, tragedy, _____

3. business, manufacturing, _____

4. soon, yesterday, _____

5. silly, amusing, _____

6. hint, recommend, _____

7. raincoat, galoshes, _____

8. quiet, soft-spoken, _____

9. await, look for, _____

10. cupboard, closet, _____

E **Sentence Sense.** Find a list word which will complete the following sentences. The word's definition is given in parentheses.

1. We will meet at four (of the clock) _____ .

2. The (gathering) _____ will begin at noon.

3. The (cupboard) _____ holds our figurine collection.

4. He owns a shoe-making (manufacturing business) _____ .

5. There is (a tropical fruit) _____ in the salad.

6. We (just before now) _____ bought a house.

7. We received a (message through wires) _____ .

8. Our family usually uses the (made from flax) _____ tablecloths

   for special guests.

F **Double Consonants.** When dividing a word that has a double consonant into syllables, you will usually divide between the double consonant. Rewrite the following words in syllables. Use your Glossary, if needed.

attic _____   assembly _____

suggest _____   umbrella _____

6

Short vowels. Circle the words below which have short vowel sounds.

radical	obey	eight	choice
general	which	Scripture	sudden
raised	taste	rejoice	hopping
lose	citizen	captain	

H **Did You Know?** Some of our words have interesting origins. Find the list word indicated by each description below. Draw a picture of the items in the margin.

1. This word comes from Attica, a region in Greece known for its architecture. It was originally a low space above the main story, indicated by the structure of the building. Now it is any low space, often for storage.

2. This word comes from a word which means to shade, because originally it was used to protect from the hot sun. In fact, it was like a large fan on a long, flexible pole. The one who carried it often walked behind an important person and kept it over his head. Today, it is a protection from rain as well.

3. This word in Portuguese means a grinning face. The Portuguese explorers who found this fruit noticed it was about the size of a head. The three dark, hollow spaces in it suggested a smile; so, they called it a grinning face.

I **Write About It.** The school year has just started. Have you thought about what you would like to accomplish this year? You need to have goals, or you will have nothing at which to aim. Think about it. What would you like to accomplish? See if you can come up with three goals for yourself. They could be related to school, home, or church. They may result in spiritual or personal growth. Write them below in complete sentences.

1. _____

_____

2. _____

_____

3. _____

_____

Be sure to enter your Home Base Words each week in the Word Bank section of your Glossary. Also, you will need to record results of First Look and the Final Evaluation on the graph in the back of the book.

truly
motivate
freeze
midnight
decided
frightened
view
envelope
value
kindnesses
supreme
beneath
details
dining
cocoa
handwriting
deacon
ideal
fellowship
unlikely

A **Work With Your Words**. This week's words have a long vowel somewhere in the word, usually in the accented syllable. Group your words below according to the long vowel sound. Two of your words have two long vowels. Draw lines and include your Home Base Words. Circle the vowel or vowels which make the long sound.

long o (as in *oats*)

long e (as in *even*)

long i (as in *idea*)

long a (as in *ate*)

long u and oo (as in *use* and *too*)

Notice the way the long vowels are spelled in the words above. Fill in the generalizations they follow.

1. In a vowel-consonant-e pattern, the vowel is _____,

   and the e is _____ .

2. When two vowels are together, the first is _____,

   and the second is _____ .

3. In an open syllable, the vowel is _____ .

B Locating Words and Respelling.

Locating Words and Respelling. The guide words in a dictionary or glossary help you locate words quickly. The guide words are the first and last words on a page. Any words which come alphabetically between the guide words would appear on that particular page. Below are pairs of guide words. Alphabetize your words under the correct pairs of guide words.

account - essay	fat - kitten	middle- wagon

Write the words shown by the dictionary respellings.

dīn´ ing _____   val´ ū _____

frēz _____   kō´ kō _____

Locate your words in the Word Find.

Write two list words suggested by the story in Daniel 5:5-6.

_____

_____

```
D E M E R P U S F N O C A E D
F R I G H T E N E D V A L U E
R I D V A L U N L I K E L Y D
E G N I N I D O L A E D I L I
E V I E W A O C O C O A V U C
Z R G N I T I R W D N A H R E
E T H M O T I V S A E D I T D
M O T I V A T E H T A E N E B
S E S S E N D N I K I N D I M
D E T A I L S E P O L E V N E
```

Reminder: Add your Home Base Words to your Glossary.

truly
motivate
freeze
midnight
decided
frightened
view
envelope
value
kindnesses
supreme
beneath
details
dining
cocoa
handwriting
deacon
ideal
fellowship
unlikely

C **Glossary Glimpse.** Decide which word or words are being described. Use your Glossary if you need to.

1. These two words end in ly.

   _____   _____

2. These two words have a long i sound spelled igh.

   _____   _____

3. These two words are compounds.

   _____   _____

4. Drop the final l on this word and you will have an *idea*.

   _____

5. *Envelop* is a verb which means to wrap. Which word is a noun which means a wrapper or container for letters?

   _____

6. Write the verb root for each noun.

   a. motivation _____

   b. decision _____

   c. writings _____

   What happened to the final e in the verb when it was changed to a noun?

   _____

7. These two words are plurals.

   _____   _____

8. This word has a double letter which is a vowel.

   _____

9. These two words have double consonants.

   _____   _____

A good dictionary or glossary is one of the most important keys to gaining word power. Use it and you'll become STRONG!

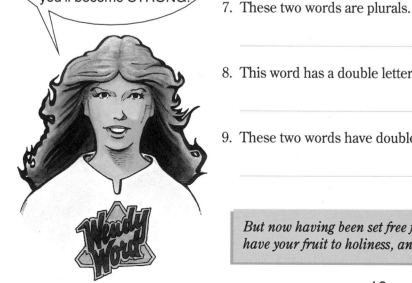

But now having been set free from sin, and having become slaves of God, you have your fruit to holiness, and the end, everlasting life. (Romans 6:22)

freeze
view
value
supreme
beneath
dining
cocoa

D **Use Your Words.** Choose from the word box to complete each sentence below.

1. The bank vault was _____ the bank.

2. Jim is _____ at a fancy restaurant tonight.

3. You will _____ if you go out in the snow without a coat.

4. We will have hot _____ for breakfast.

5. Nebuchadnezzar was the _____ ruler of Babylon.

6. Of what _____ is it, if you gain the whole world, but lose your own soul?

7. The family room has a beautiful _____ of the skyline.

E **Did You Know?** *Deacon* comes from the Greek word *diakonos* meaning a servant. In Acts 6:1-8, seven deacons were chosen to serve tables so the apostles could spend more time in the ministry of the Gospel. Those who later served as deacons were also recognized as officers in the church. Paul listed their qualifications in I Timothy 3. We can conclude that deacons not only served tables, but also helped the ministry in any way they could, as servants. Jesus said, "Where I am, there shall also my servant (*diakonos*) be" (John 12:26). In that respect, all Christians are to be *deacons* (servants) of Christ.

F **Write About It.** How can you be Christ's servant? Think about some things you can do for Him as a young person. You can serve Him at home, school, church, and in the neighborhood. Write about some of the ways you can serve Him.

_____

_____

_____

_____

_____

neither
height
foreign
chillier
freight
pier
relieve
easier
buried
received
studied
beige
weird
shield
empties
weighed
achieve
fiercely
unbelief
neighborly

A **Work With Your Words.** Each of the following words needs an ie or ei to complete it. Fill in the ie or ei within the word; then rewrite the word on the line provided. Not all the words are from your list.

1. fr _____ ght _____

2. h _____ ght _____

3. w _____ rd _____

4. n _____ ther _____

5. rel _____ ve _____

6. for _____ gn _____

7. b _____ ge _____

8. sh _____ ld _____

9. p _____ r _____

10. ch _____ f _____

11. f _____ ld _____

12. prev _____ w _____

Write the list word that is related to each of the following words. For example, the list word related to *easy* is *easier*.

1. belief _____

2. achievement _____

3. neighbor _____

4. receive _____

5. weigh _____

6. fierce _____

7. empty _____

8. student _____

But as many as received him, to them He gave the right to become children of God, to those who believe in his name. (John 1:12)

12

B **I Before E or E Before I?** Many of your words contain an ie or ei which usually follows the generalization: "I before e, except after c, or when sounded as a long a." Write six of your list words that are spelled with ie on the lines below. Check yes if the word is spelled according to the generalization. Check no if it is not. (For example, *view* from Lesson 2 follows the generalization because i comes before e.)

		yes	no
1.			
2.			
3.			
4.			
5.			
6.			

Use ___ before ___ , except after ___ , or when sounded as a long ___ .

Write your words that are spelled with ei on the lines below. Follow the same directions as above.

		yes	no
1.			
2.			
3.			
4.			
5.			
6.			
7.			
8.			
9.			

Don't forget! Add your Home Base Words to your Glossary.

neither
height
foreign
chillier
freight
pier
relieve
easier
buried
received
studied
beige
weird
shield
empties
weighed
achieve
fiercely
unbelief
neighborly

Acrostic Action. Fill in the acrostic below, using one of your words for each clue. The letters in the boxes going down will spell a word which means lack of belief.

Clues
1. hid in the ground
2. not either
3. tan in color
4. strange
5. reduce pain
6. landing place for boats
7. cargo
8. from another country

1. □

2. □

3. □

4. □

5. □

6. □

7. □

8. □

Roots That Change. Some of your words are from root words that end in y. Write the five words and their roots. (Example: *countries — country*)

1. _____ _____
2. _____ _____
3. _____ _____
4. _____ _____
5. _____ _____

A Little-Known Fact.
Height is one of only a few English words where eigh is pronounced long i. Remember that it is related to other words of measurement like *eight*, *weight*, and *freight*.

Q: What would you have to do to each root word that ends in y following a consonant to change it to a list word?

A: Change the _____ to _____ before adding the new ending.

E **Did You Know?** According to the Jews, a *foreigner* was anyone who was not a Jew. That would make all of us foreigners, unless we happen to be Jewish. Israelites could not marry foreigners, nor make covenants with them. Foreigners were not permitted to participate in some Jewish privileges. They could not eat the Passover, enter the sanctuary or become king. Jesus changed all that. Christ's death was for all, foreigners as well as Jews. Now, as Christians, we are no longer foreigners, but citizens with all the other saints. We are part of God's family (Ephesians 2:19).

F **Write About It**. When Paul and Silas were in jail, they praised God. An earthquake shook the doors open and they were free. The jailer was ready to kill himself because he was responsible for all the prisoners. What a relief to find the prisoners still there! He asked Paul and Silas a critical question: What must I do to be saved?

Mary, how do you know you are saved?

I'm glad you asked....

The answer was simple: "_____ on the Lord Jesus Christ, and you shall be saved and your house" (Acts 16:25-34). Find and read the following verses: Romans 3:23; Romans 6:23; and Romans 10:9-10. Think about leading someone to Christ. Write below what you would tell someone who asks you how to be saved. Use some of your spelling words and Home Base Words, if possible.

_____

_____

_____

_____

_____

_____

_____

_____

_____

_____

Don't forget to mark your scores from First Look and Final Evaluation on the graph in the back of your spelling book.

couple
account
ought
saucer
compound
countries
coffee
foster
laughter
chalkboard
doubtful
naughty
downstream
could've
how's
automotive
calming
alternate
roughly
would've

A **Work With Your Words**. Vowel digraphs are two vowels that combine to make their own sound. All of this week's words have vowel digraphs. The vowels combine to make one of several sounds. Place your words in the correct area based on the vowel sound. Draw lines and add Home Base Words.

These words have the au sound as in *caught*. This sound can be spelled au, aw, a(l), augh, ough, or o.

These words have the ou sound as in *out*. The sound is spelled ou or ow.

These words have the short oo sound as in *wood*. The sound is spelled ou.

These words have the short u sound as in *fun*. The sound is spelled ou.

This word has the short a sound as in *hat*. The sound is spelled au. It is the only common English word spelled this way.

A merry heart does good, like medicine.
(Proverbs 17:22)

B **Analyze Your Words.**

1. Several of your words have silent letters. Find your words as described below and write them on the lines provided.

   a. silent b   _____

   b. silent l after a   _____   _____

   c. silent l after ou   _____   _____

   d. silent gh   _____   _____

2. Write the words which have the following suffixes:

   a. ly   _____

   b. ing   _____

   c. ful   _____

3. This word has a long e spelled ea.   _____

4. This word has a double consonant and a double vowel.   _____

5. This word is a plural. Write its singular form.   _____

6. These two words are compounds.

   _____   _____

C **Interesting Origins.** Several of your words have interesting backgrounds. Write the word that is described under its matching picture.

1. This dish held sauces which were used to flavor meat. Now it holds a cup, but it was too expensive to make it for such an insignificant task when it was first used in 1340.

   _____

2. This was originally quicklime, from the Latin words *calx vive* (living lime). Lime was used as mortar. Today this substance is used for writing or drawing.

   _____

3. These beans were originally chewed because they caused a person to be more active and full of energy. Today, the beans are brewed to make a dark brown drink.

   _____

couple
account
ought
saucer
compound
countries
coffee
foster
laughter
chalkboard
doubtful
naughty
downstream
could've
how's
automotive
calming
alternate
roughly
would've

D **Find A Rhyme**. Find your words which rhyme with the following words. Be careful: Sometimes the spelling changes.

1. caught _____   2. toffee _____

3. roster _____   4. supple _____

5. gruffly _____   6. cows _____

7. should've _____

E **Make A Contraction**. A contraction is a shortened word made by putting two words together. One or more letters are left out, and an apostrophe is placed where the letters were. Make contractions of the following phrases.
For example: *are + not = aren't*

1. could + have = _____

2. should + have = _____

3. would + have = _____

4. how + is = _____

5. who + is = _____

6. she + has = _____

7. it + is = _____

F **The Sound Of F**. The f sound can be spelled several ways. Circle the letters which spell the f sound in the following words. Then write the word on the line.

1. roughly _____   2. phone _____

3. foster _____   4. coffee _____

5. laughter _____   6. doubtful _____

7. graph _____   8. enough _____

9. proof _____   10. phrase _____

In two of your list words, gh is pronounced f. Write them.

_____   _____

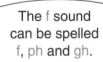

The f sound can be spelled f, ph and gh.

Don't forget to add your Home Base Words to your Glossary.

G **Did You Know?** Isaac was born to Abraham and Sarah in their old age. His name means "one laughs." That seems like a strange name for a baby, but it was an appropriate name. God told Abraham that he was going to have a son. Abraham laughed because he was 100 years old! An angel told Abraham again that he would have a son. Sarah was listening, and heard the news also. Her reaction was the same as Abraham's. She laughed because she was 90 years old! When the son was born, he was named Isaac. Sarah said it was because God made her laugh and all that heard would laugh with her. The laughter was not because of how ridiculous it seemed to be having a child in old age, but because of the great joy they experienced in having a son. Surely, many others would share their joy and laugh with them.

H **Write About It**. The Bible says, "A merry heart makes a cheerful countenance." When we are happy on the inside, we show it on the outside. The Scripture also says, "A merry heart does good, like medicine." When we are feeling a little low, someone else can lift our spirits by making us laugh. Think of a time when you were feeling sad and someone else came along and lifted your spirits. Or, maybe it was the other way around: Someone else was sad and you lifted his or her spirits. Tell what happened, using some of your spelling words and Home Base Words.

Record your scores.

magazines
museum
rare
novels
catalog
students
nonfiction
references
legends
literature
essays
checkout
volumes
biographies
fined
mysteries
shelving
historical
binders
stacks

A **Work With Your Words**. Design a floor plan for a <u>library</u>. The book shelves are all along the four walls. One wall is <u>fiction</u>, but is divided into <u>historical</u>, <u>Christian</u>, <u>mysteries</u>, <u>novels</u> and <u>general fiction</u>. Another wall is <u>nonfiction</u>, divided into <u>biographies</u>, <u>science</u>, <u>religion</u>, <u>essay collections</u>, <u>literature</u> and <u>legends</u>. The third wall is <u>references</u>, and is divided into <u>encyclopedias</u>, <u>almanacs</u> and <u>general references</u>. The fourth wall has a small <u>display section</u> and a section of <u>magazines</u>. Somewhere in the middle, you need to draw a space for the <u>checkout desk</u>, the <u>card catalogs</u> and a <u>dictionary stand</u>. Label each area underlined above.

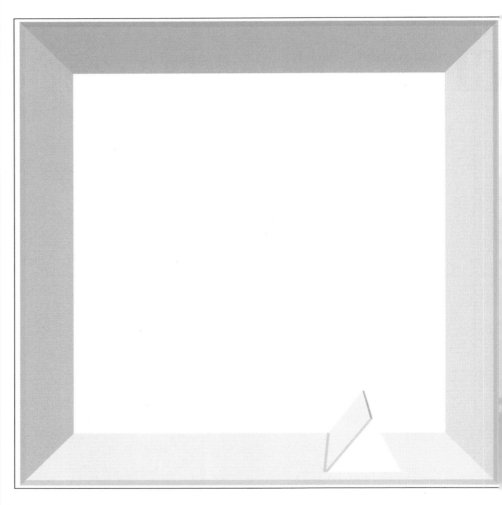

B **Where To Look**. Tell what section to go to in the library to find each of the following:

1. a mystery _____

2. <u>National</u> <u>Geographic</u> _____

3. a book about a real person _____

4. a fiction book based on the Civil War _____

5. information about planets _____

C **Dictionary Delight**. Below is a sample of a dictionary page. Use it to answer the questions which follow.

SUPER!
LESSON
5

checkout   legends

checkout check out (chek′ out) adj., n. 1. the place for settling purchases *The checkout lane was crowded due to the sale.* 2. the place in a library for settling which books can be taken *We went to the checkout to get three books.*

essays es says (es′ āz) n. nonfiction articles which give the author's viewpoint *The essays about homework were due last week.*

fined (fīnd) v. punished by a fine *She was fined 25 cents for the late book.*

historical his tor i cal (his tȯr′ i kəl) adj. having to do with or based on history *Historical facts can help us solve problems today.*

legends leg ends (lej′ əndz) n. stories shared and passed down from one generation to another which are accepted as true, but cannot be checked *We read several legends in class.*

1. What are the guide words for this page?

_____

_____

2. What is the first entry on this page?

_____

3. What is the last entry on this page?

_____

4. What part tells you how to divide the word into

syllables? _____

5. How do you know how to pronounce the word?

_____

6. Which word has two definitions?

_____

7. What do each of the following stand for?

n.   _____

v.   _____

adj. _____

8. What is the part of speech for each of these:

fined   _____

legends _____

historical _____

9. Which word means nonfiction articles?

_____

10. Which word means punished by a fine?

_____

D **Homophones.** *Fined* means punished by a *fine*, and *find* means to recover something which was lost. *Found* is the past tense of *find*. Use these words correctly in the following sentences.

1. Did you _____ your hat?

2. The judge _____ the speeder $50.

3. Terry _____ his ball under the shrubbery.

4. Joey paid a _____ for overdue books.

5. I wonder if Dr. Kienel has _____ his glasses.

6. I cannot _____ my keys.

#50 FINE!

magazines
museum
rare
novels
catalog
students
nonfiction
references
legends
literature
essays
checkout
volumes
biographies
fined
mysteries
shelving
historical
binders
stacks

 Analyze Your Words.

1. List the words which are plurals. Add any of your Home Base Words which are plural.

_____   _____   _____

_____   _____   _____

_____   _____   _____

  a. How were plurals made for most of your words? Add _____ to make most words plural.

  b. Write the root word for *biographies* and *mysteries*.

_____   _____

What did you do to these two word endings to make them plural? Change the

_____ to _____ and add _____ .

  c. Write the root word for *essays*. _____ Why don't you change the y to i in this word? Fill in the generalization.

If a _____ comes before the _____ , keep the _____ . If

a _____ comes before the _____ , change the _____ to

_____ and add es.

2. An alternate spelling for one of your words is *catalogue*. How is it spelled in

your list? _____

3. *Reference* comes from the word _____ . Don't forget the middle syllable. Write the word twice.

_____   _____

4. What is the root word for *shelving*? _____ What do you do to the

root to make shelving? Change the _____ to _____ and add

_____ .

5. How many syllables are in *literature*? _____ Don't forget the second

syllable. Pronouncing the word correctly can help you remember how to

spell it. Write the word twice.

_____   _____

The library is full of sources to help you gain Word Power. Get to know and use them all!

F **Compounds**. Compounds are two words put together to make one new word. They can be written one of three different ways: 1) Two words together as in *drawbridge*; 2) Two words joined with a hyphen as in *town-clerk*; or 3) Two words separated as in *wise men*. Write the following compounds correctly. Use a dictionary if you are unsure.

earth
quake _____

high
minded _____

type
writer _____

wrist
watch _____

ice
cream _____

post
office _____

corner
stone _____

check
out _____

self
control _____

thanks
giving _____

The word *checkout* has a different form for the verb, *check out*. Write in the correct verb form for this sentence.

I _____ _____ four books from the library yesterday.

G **Did You Know?** We usually think of a *mystery* as something we cannot explain or for which we have no answer. This is not so in the Bible. Paul used the word frequently to mean a truth which was concealed but is now revealed in the Gospel.

H **Write About It**. Pretend you are one of the first-century apostles like Peter, Paul or James. You are writing to a friend to reveal the mystery of the Gospel of Christ. This friend cannot understand how you can say Christ is a man and is also God. Tell this friend several things about Christ which prove He is man; then tell him several things Christ did which prove He is God. You may want to start your letter with a greeting similar to those of the apostles. Check Galatians 1:1-3, Ephesians 1:1-2, James 1:1 or II Peter 1:1.

_____

_____

_____

_____

_____

_____

Be sure to enter your Home Base Words and scores in their appropriate areas in the back of your book.

couple
magazines
expect
truly
o'clock
motivate
neither
height
ought
freeze
saucer
electric
view
museum
rare
attic
umbrella
freight
novels
catalog
relieve
received
dining
how's
would've

A **Short Vowels and Consonants Review**.

1. Write at least two words with the following short vowel sounds. Several words have more than one short vowel.

short a as in *hat* _____ _____ _____

short e as in *egg* _____ _____ _____

short i as in *it* _____ _____ _____

short o as in *hot* _____ _____ _____

short u as in *up* _____ _____ _____

2. Write the words with the following consonants.

ck says k _____   x says ks _____

c says k _____

_____ _____ _____

B **Long Vowel Review**. Write the words with the following long vowel sounds. Sometimes more than one word has the long vowel sound.

long a as in *ate* _____

long e as in *even* _____

_____

_____

long i as in *idea* _____

long o as in *oats* _____   long oo as in *blue* _____

long u as in *use* _____

Principles Review. Remember the way long vowel sounds are spelled in Lesson 2. Fill in the generalizations they follow.

1. In a vowel-consonant-e pattern, the vowel is

_____, and the e is _____.

2. When two vowels are together, the first is

_____, and the second is _____.

3. In an open syllable, the vowel is _____.

C **Review the ie/ei Generalization.**

1. Write the ie /ei generalization.

Use _____ before _____ , except after _____ , or when sounded as a long _____ .

2. Write list words which follow the ie /ei generalization. Then think
   of another word which follows the same generalization and write it.

   i comes before e _____ _____

   ei follows a c _____ _____

   ei says ā _____ _____

You first!

3. Write the two words which do not follow the generalization.

   ei says ī _____   ei says ē _____

4. Write the root word for each of the following. Be careful. You may
   need to make a change in spelling.

   chillier _____   buried _____

   received _____   easier _____

   studied _____   weighed _____

When a root word ends in y following a consonant, change the _____ to _____ before adding the ending.

D **Vowel Digraph Review.**

1. A vowel digraph is two _____ combined to make their

   own _____ .

"We *ought* to obey God rather
than men."

2. Write your words with the following vowel digraphs.

   au sound as in *caught* _____

   ou sound as in *out* _____

   oo sound as in *should* _____

   u sound as in *fun* _____

couple
magazines
expect
truly
o'clock
motivate
neither
height
ought
freeze
saucer
electric
view
museum
rare
attic
umbrella
freight
novels
catalog
relieve
received
dining
how's
would've

E **Contraction Subtraction.**

A _____ is a shortened word made by putting two words together and leaving out one or more letters. An _____ is placed where the letters were left out.

Make contractions of the following.

could + have = _____   would + have = _____

it + is = _____   she + has = _____

F **Revisiting the Library.** Match the following descriptions with list words.

something you could read _____

_____ a listing of names, etc. _____

a building with displays _____ not common _____

G **Same and Different.** Amy Antonym represents words that are different in the first column. Sam Synonym represents words that are the same in the second column.

basement _____   sincerely _____

thaw _____   parasol _____

depth _____   periodicals _____

gave _____   should _____

common _____   two _____

H **Word Study.** Find list words which match the following descriptions.

These have a silent gh. _____ _____

These have a c which says s. _____

These are plurals. _____ _____

26

I **Did You Know?** *Electric* comes from the Greek word *elektron*, which was actually *amber*, a fossil resin which becomes full of static electricity when it is rubbed. When other objects were found to have this same static electricity, they were said to have the characteristics of amber. Thus, they came to be known as *electric*. Combine *electric* with a noun and write the two-word phrases below.

electric _____ skillet _____ _____ _____

_____ _____ _____ _____

_____ _____ _____ _____

J **Crossword Puzzle**. Do the crossword puzzle using the clues and your Glossary, if needed.

ACROSS
1. BUILDING TO DISPLAY OBJECTS
4. OF THE CLOCK
5. CARGO
6. WOULD HAVE
7. EATING DINNER
9. POWERED BY CURRENT
11. SIGHT, VISION
14. REDUCE PAIN
15. LONG FICTION STORIES

DOWN
2. SHALLOW DISH
3. URGE ON
8. NOT EITHER
10. LIST OF TITLES IN LIBRARY
12. LOOK FOR
13. HOW IS

There's nothing like a good review to build your word-power muscles.

K **Write About It**. Choose one of the following topics and write a story using at least ten of your spelling words from the first five lessons. Use your own paper and draw at least one picture to go with the story.

The Old Umbrella in the Attic

A Catalog From 400 B.C.

The View From the Saucer

Dining in a Space Ship

choices
anyway
destroy
enjoyable
joint
employ
prayer
daily
prepaid
annoy
faint
survey
raisin
repay
alley
royalty
betrayal
volleyball
joined
obeyed

A **Work With Your Words**. All of this week's words contain a vowel digraph: oi, oy, ai, ay or ey. Group your words below according to the sound and spelling of the vowel digraph. Draw lines and add your Home Base Words where they belong.

oi spelled oi as in *oil*

oi spelled oy as in *joy*

long a spelled ai as in *aid*

long a spelled ay as in *day*

long a spelled ey as in *they*

long e spelled ey as in *valley*

ayer becomes er as in *errand*

B **Homophones**. A *feint* is a fake swing in boxing to catch the opponent off guard. Use this word and its homophone from the list in the following sentence.

Uppercut Calhoun's _____ was so convincing that it

made Weak Knee Willy _____.

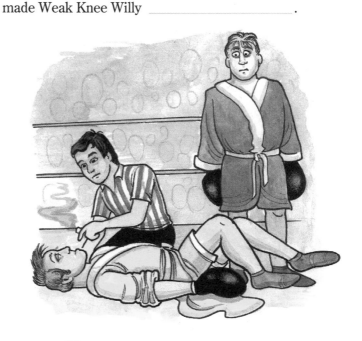

28

C **Rhymes**. Find one or more of your words to rhyme with each of the following:

1. rally _____

2. paint _____

3. voices _____

4. loyalty _____

5. point _____

6. coined _____

7. enjoy _____ _____ _____

Think of as many words as you can that rhyme with *care*. Write them on the lines. You should be able to think of at least five. One of them is a list word, but is not spelled like *care*.

_____

_____

D **Antonyms, Synonyms, and Definitions**. Find a list word which is an antonym for each of the following. Write the word on the line.

1. create _____

2. yearly _____

3. charged _____

4. disobeyed _____

Find a list word which is a synonym for each of the following. Write the word on the line.

1. pleasant _____

2. selections _____

3. deceit _____

4. anyhow _____

Find one of your words to match each of the following definitions.

1. examine carefully _____

2. act of talking to God _____

3. pay back _____

4. dried grape _____

Here are some guides to help you divide syllables:

1. Separate prefixes and suffixes.
2. Make sure every syllable has a vowel.
3. Separate between consonants.
4. Separate after long vowels and vowel digraphs.

E **Syllable Division**. Divide the following words into syllables. Write the word on the line and leave a space between syllables. Use your Glossary, if needed.

1. enjoyable _____

2. betrayal _____

3. annoy _____

4. employ _____

choices
anyway
destroy
enjoyable
joint
employ
prayer
daily
prepaid
annoy
faint
survey
raisin
repay
alley
royalty
betrayal
volleyball
joined
obeyed

F **Analyze Your Words.**

1. Find two words which are compounds.

   _____ _____

2. Write two words which have *join* as the root. Tell the part of speech for each.

   _____ _____

3. Find words with the following suffixes:

   al _____   ty _____

   able _____   s _____

   ed _____

4. Write two words which have *pay* as their root.

   _____ _____

   Re means *back*. What does *repay* mean?

   _____

   Pre means *before*. What does *prepaid* mean?

   _____

   Notice what happened to *pay* when it became past tense. Make the following words past tense in the same way.

   say _____   lay _____

   These words rhyme in the present tense. Do they rhyme in the past tense?

G **Picture This.** Write the word for each picture.

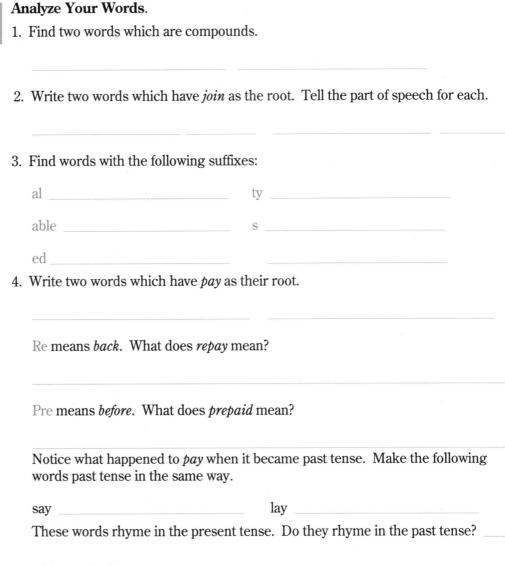

1. _____   2. _____   3. _____

4. _____   5. _____

Write in two more words and draw pictures for them.

_____ _____

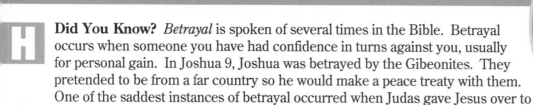

H **Did You Know?** *Betrayal* is spoken of several times in the Bible. Betrayal occurs when someone you have had confidence in turns against you, usually for personal gain. In Joshua 9, Joshua was betrayed by the Gibeonites. They pretended to be from a far country so he would make a peace treaty with them. One of the saddest instances of betrayal occurred when Judas gave Jesus over to the Jewish authorities for thirty pieces of silver. Contrast this with loyalty and friendship. David and Jonathan were so selfless in their concern for one another that they were willing to sacrifice their lives for each other. But the greatest display of loyalty and friendship was when Jesus laid down His life for us at Calvary.

Joshua 9

I **Write About It.** Has anyone ever betrayed you? Perhaps you had a best friend who decided to choose someone else. Perhaps someone spread false rumors about you. Write about a time when you were deeply hurt because of the way you were treated. Or it could be that you have deeply hurt someone else by your actions and need to write about that experience.

_____

_____

_____

_____

_____

Now, try to think of a time when someone was loyal enough to put your needs and interests ahead of his or her own. Perhaps that person became a good friend because he or she supported you at a time when everyone else seemed to be against you. Tell what happened.

I Samuel 19

_____

_____

_____

_____

_____

_____

Romans 5:8

Don't forget to add your Home Base Words to the Glossary. Use your Word Bank anytime that you need some spelling assistance. Also be sure to record your scores for this lesson.

Target: Long **u** and **oo**

continued
avenue
produce
canoe
perfume
beauty
regular
popular
jewels
rescue
bruised
pursuit
nephew
loosen
Europe
losing
congratulate
argue
included
fruitful

 Work With Your Words. All of this week's words contain the sound of long u as in *use*, or the long oo as in *cool*. These two sounds are very similar and can be spelled in a variety of ways. Place your words in the word forms below.

Note the shaded boxes. You will need to especially study these spellings. List the ten ways to spell the long oo and u sounds.

B **Where In the World?** Identify the continents on the map by writing the name of the continent and its abbreviation on the line by the correct number. For example, if number one is South America, write South America and its abbreviation next to number one. Use the following abbreviations: *N.A., S.A., Eur., Ant., Aust.,* and *Afr.* (There is no abbreviation for *Asia*.)

1. _____

2. _____

3. _____

4. _____

5. _____

6. _____

7. _____

C **Street Signs.** Make up a street name for each of the signs. Write the correct abbreviations for the names you choose. Use each of the following: *Street, Avenue, Court, Road,* and *Boulevard.*

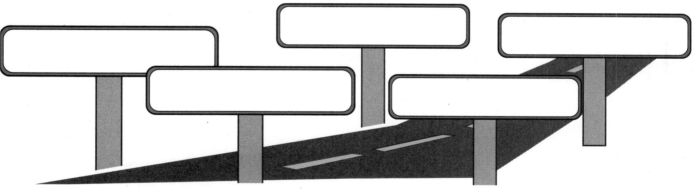

D **Titles.** Give each of the people pictured a title using the correct abbreviation. Use each title only once. Choose from the following: *Captain, Doctor, Miss, Mister,* and *Reverend.* Make up a last name to go along with the title.

continued
avenue
produce
canoe
perfume
beauty
regular
popular
jewels
rescue
bruised
pursuit
nephew
loosen
Europe
losing
congratulate
argue
included
fruitful

Lost Vowels. Fill in the missing vowels in each of the words below. Then rewrite the word on the line provided.

1. p __ p __ l __ r _____

2. fr __ __ t f __ l _____

3. b __ __ __ t y _____

4. __ n c l __ d __ d _____

5. r __ s c __ __ _____

6. br __ __ s __ d _____

7. __ r g __ __ _____

8. c __ n __ __ __ _____

9. c __ n t __ n __ __ d _____

10. p __ r s __ __ t _____

Don't Lose Your Loose Tooth. *Loose* and *lose* are often confused. *Loose* means not tight, and *lose* means misplace. *Lose* has one s, just like its related word, *lost*. Look at the following picture clues to help you remember the words; then use the correct word in each sentence below.

1. She has a _____ tooth.

2. You will _____ it, if you don't put it in a safe place.

3. If they _____ this game, they will not be in the play-offs.

4. Our pet hamster got _____ last night.

Already Happened. Past tense means something has already happened. Often words which are past tense end in ed. Write three of your words which are past tense.

_____ _____

Write the past tense form of the following verbs.

1. argue _____   2. produce _____

3. rescue _____   4. congratulate _____

34

 Did You Know? *Perfume* was important in Bible times. It was sometimes used as a holy anointing oil. Moses was commanded by God to make a perfume and anoint the tabernacle, the ark, several tabernacle pieces, and Aaron and his sons (Exodus 30:22-33).

Perfumes were also used to prepare women for marriage, anoint respected people and embalm the dead. Jesus was anointed with very expensive perfume by Mary just before His death (John 12:1-8). Several women had prepared perfume to anoint Jesus' body. They came to His tomb, but found it empty (Luke 23:56-24:3). Our prayers are like perfume to God. Revelation tells us God saves the prayers of Christians in small containers to be poured out on the altar before His throne (Revelation 5:8 and 8:3-4).

Write About It. The psalmist said, "Let my prayer be set forth before You as incense." Our prayers are sweet to God when they honor Him. Write a prayer to God that you would consider a sweet smell. Perhaps it will be a prayer of praise and adoration, telling Him how wonderful He is.

Date: _____

_____

_____

_____

_____

_____

_____

_____

Don't forget! Add your Home Base Words to your Word Bank and record your scores.

calendars
grammar
chapter
collar
burst
squirrel
pattern
curved
deserve
standard
nervous
particular
salary
pearls
earnestly
journalist
groceries
fervent
searching
answering

A **Work With Your Words**. All of this week's words have an r following a vowel somewhere in the word. This combination often produces a schwa r sound. This sound can be spelled several different ways. Place your words in the correct column below based on the spelling of the schwa r sound.

ar as in *suga*r

er as in *river*

ear as in *earn*

ur as in *curtain*

ir as in *dirty*

our as in *journey*

The schwa r sound can be spelled several different ways. In this lesson it is spelled

_____ , _____ , _____ , _____ , _____ , and _____ .

Draw lines and add Home Base Words which have the schwa r sound.

Don't forget! Record your score for First Look on the graph in the back of your student book. Also enter your Home Base Words in the Glossary.

B **Sound Check**. Circle the words below which contain the schwa r sound.

worth	honor	parents	borrow
pour	shower	software	argue
armor	purple	serve	bruise
banner	carols	fever	curtain

C **All Things in Order**. Put the following list words in alphabetical order. Remember that you may have to look at the second or third letter to alphabetize correctly.

deserve
pearls
collar
grammar
squirrel
burst
groceries
journalist
answering
earnestly
calendars
particular

1. _____

2. _____

3. _____

4. _____

5. _____

6. _____

7. _____

8. _____

9. _____

10. _____

11. _____

12. _____

D **Meanings Match**. Match the following words with the correct definition. You may need to use the Glossary.

pattern	standard	nervous	salary
curved	chapter	fervent	searching

1. showing emotional strain or tension _____

2. bent; moved in a bending path _____

3. a model or form used as a guide _____

4. wage; a fixed amount of pay _____

5. exploring; looking for something _____

6. a level of excellence _____

7. a section of a book _____

8. hot, glowing; intense _____

calendars
grammar
chapter
collar
burst
squirrel
pattern
curved
deserve
standard
nervous
particular
salary
pearls
earnestly
journalist
groceries
fervent
searching
answering

E **Rhymes**. Write a list word which rhymes with each of the following words. Be careful of spellings. Sometimes the same sound is spelled differently.

Saturn _____   calorie _____

service _____   served _____

hammer _____   curls _____

worst _____   dollar _____

perching _____   servant _____

F **Picture This**. Look at each picture; then write the list word.

1. "nervous"

2. salary

3. s(ear)ching

4. curved

5. collar

6. PEARLS

7. GROCERIES

8. BURST

1. _____
2. _____
3. _____
4. _____
5. _____
6. _____
7. _____
8. _____

Draw two pictures of your Home Base Words and have someone write the word by the picture.

G **Did You Know?** *Salary* comes from the word *salt*. Long ago, when a Roman soldier received his salary, he used it to purchase salt. Even then, salt was known to be essential for good health. If a soldier was not worth his salt, he was worthless, not deserving of a salary, or salt allowance.

H **Word Search**. The following words are hidden in the Word Search below. Circle them, and then write them on the lines provided.

| deserve | standard | chapter | groceries | calendars |
| particular | journalist | answering | earnestly | squirrel |

```
J  O  U  R  N  A  L  I  S  T  P
G  A  E  B  C  D  E  C  E  G  A
R  S  V  F  G  H  I  A  A  N  R
O  Q  R  J  K  L  M  L  R  I  T
C  U  E  N  O  P  Q  E  N  R  I
E  I  S  R  S  T  T  N  E  E  C
R  R  E  U  V  P  W  D  S  W  U
I  R  D  R  A  D  N  A  T  S  L
E  E  X  H  Y  Z  A  R  L  N  A
S  L  C  B  E  D  E  S  Y  A  R
```

_____

_____

_____

_____

_____

_____

_____

I **Searching Scripture**. Acts tells us the Bereans received the Word gladly and searched it daily. Psalm 119:100 says we can have more understanding than the people of long ago because we have God's Word available to us. What else do we receive as a result of focusing our minds on Scripture? Name at least three things from Psalm 119:49-56 and 97-105.

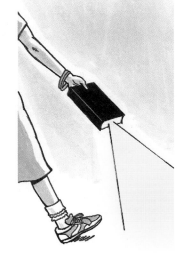

_____

_____

_____

J **Write About It**. Psalm 119 takes 176 verses to tell the wonders of God's Word. David felt it to be very special! Why is it so special, and what does it mean to you?

_____

_____

_____

_____

worst
orbit
normal
major
effort
source
therefore
depository
afford
harbor
anchor
chores
incorrect
factory
survivor
comfort
evaporate
satisfactory
trustworthy
sorrowful

 A **Work With Your Words**. All of this week's words have an or somewhere in the word. This combination produces one of three sounds. Place your words in the correct column below based on the or sound.

1. or says ər as in *color*

2. or says ȯr as in *sort*

our says ȯr as in *sort* _____

3. or says är as in *borrow* _____

Isn't this a nice O-R-bit!

Three of your words have two r-controlled vowels. Find the three words which fit the following descriptions.

ere says er as in *errand* _____

ar says är as in *arm* _____

ur says ər as in *turtle* _____

B Choose a Word. The following story, taken from Acts 27, has several blanks for you to fill in. Places with a blue line must be filled in with one of your list words. Places with a red line may be filled in with a word of your choice. Try to use some Home Base Words.

As Paul, the apostle, was nearing the end of his ministry, he was sent to Rome

to appear before Caesar as a prisoner. Paul and several other prisoners were placed in the care of a

centurion, and they headed for Italy.

When it got _____ to winter, Paul warned them that they should stay in the

_____ because winter would make the ocean too rough for sailing. The centurion refused to

listen to Paul, raised the _____, and set sail.

The ship was _____ caught in the _____

storm of the season. After many days of tossing about, they were

_____ they would all die at sea. An angel of God _____

and assured Paul the men would all be safe, but the ship would be destroyed.

This was a source of _____.

On the fourteenth night, they thought they would be tossed onto an

island, and many sailors were ready to jump _____.

Since Paul was a _____ prisoner, the captain believed

him when he said they must all stay on board or there would be no

_____s. _____, the command

was given that no one was to escape. Paul led the men in prayer, and

they ate to regain their _____.

Soon the ship was tossed near land. It was _____

into many pieces. Since many could swim, they jumped into the water

and, with great _____, swam to land. Others

grabbed boards from the ship. Surely, God was the

_____ of their _____. All 266

were safe! What might have been a _____

situation served to confirm the power of God.

Stay with the ship and you'll be safe!

What'll we do? This storm will kill us!

worst
orbit
normal
major
effort
source
therefore
depository
afford
harbor
anchor
chores
incorrect
factory
survivor
comfort
evaporate
satisfactory
trustworthy
sorrowful

Picture This.

1. The ȯr sound is usually spelled or or ore, but in one of your words it is spelled our. Remember this: Our source of light is the sun. Don't forget to keep the u in

   source. Write *source* twice. _____

2. Two of your words are compounds. Write them.

   _____   _____

3. An *anchor* is used to keep a boat from drifting. Write the word twice.

      _____

4. A *factor* originally was a doer or maker. So, a *factory* is a place where something is made or done. *Satisfactory*, then, means made or done well. Write

   factory and *satisfactory*. _____

5. *Afford* is associated with money. This may help you remember how to spell it. Write the word twice.

        _____

6. *Survivor* comes from a Latin root, *vivus*, which means living. To *survive* means to outlive. A *survivor* is one who lives through a dangerous situation. Write the word twice.

   survivor   _____

7. Special things (like bags of money) can be kept safe in a *depository*. Write the word twice.

   depository   _____

8. *Vapor* is a mist of water changing to air. *Evaporate* means to vanish. Write the word twice.

   evaporate   _____

9. Draw two more of your words so you can remember how to spell them.

Draw your pictures here.

42

D **Write About It**. Have you ever been in a frightening situation? Perhaps it was an earthquake, or a hurricane, or a tornado. It may have been a terrible accident. How did you feel? On the lines below tell what happened and how you felt.

_____

_____

_____

_____

_____

Hopefully, you remembered to turn to the Lord for strength and comfort during your frightening experience. The Bible tells us we even have a special Comforter in the Holy Spirit. An angel of the Lord appeared to Paul with a message to comfort and encourage him. Pretend you were on Paul's ship. How would you react to this life-threatening storm?

_____

_____

_____

A w before or says wər.

E **The Word is Work**. When or follows a w, it usually has the schwa r sound as in *worst*. Circle the words below in which the or has the schwa r sound.

worthy	worship	worm	worn
word	wore	worry	worthwhile

Can you think of any other words which have a wor in them? Write five of them here. Check a dictionary if needed.

_____

_____

_____

_____

Be sure to record scores and enter your Home Base Words.

sincere
prepare
declare
carefully
period
material
ordinary
territory
interior
area
appear
admire
wearing
weary
apparent
ourselves
serious
cherish
superior
irritable

A **Work With Your Words**. All of this week's words have an r following a vowel somewhere in the word. This combination produces one of five sounds studied this week. Place your words in the correct column below based on the vowel + r sound. Two of your words go in two places.

our as in *ours*   er as in *bear*

ir as in *cereal*

ȯr as in *cord*

Ῑr as in *fire*

Two of your words have two r-controlled vowels. One of the r-controlled vowels is the schwa r sound used in a previous lesson. Write the two words below which have this schwa r sound.

Victor, I *sincerely admire* you for not becoming *irritable* with the students.

That's easy, Wendy. These fifth graders are not *ordinary* students. They *appear* to be made of *superior material!*

B **Different Words; Different Meanings.** Write words that rhyme with the following words by changing the beginning sound to the sound indicated in parentheses.

1. carefully (pr) _____

2. cherish (p) _____

Look up the following underlined words in the Glossary. Write the definition that tells what the word means in the sentence.

1. The <u>area</u> of the yard is 150 square feet. _____

_____

2. You will need three yards of <u>material</u>. _____

_____

3. Jim has a <u>serious</u> decision to make. _____

_____

4. Sam has history seventh <u>period</u>. _____

_____

5. Mom grew <u>weary</u> of the many questions of her two-year-old.

_____

6. The settlers were traveling to the Oregon <u>territory</u>.

_____

7. Sue had to <u>declare</u> purchases when she went through customs.

_____

C **Picture This.** Match one of your spelling words to the correct Word Form below by filling in the letters of your spelling word.

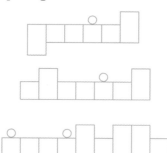
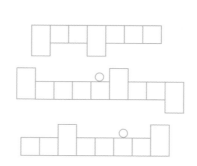
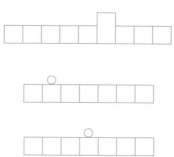

sincere
prepare
declare
carefully
period
material
ordinary
territory
interior
area
appear
admire
wearing
weary
apparent
ourselves
serious
cherish
superior
irritable

D **Word Check.** Your word list will help you find words which match the following clues. You may need to use the Glossary.

1. Antonyms are opposites.
   Write an antonym for the following.

   a. patient _____   b. vanish _____

   c. unusual _____   d. rested _____

2. Synonyms mean the same.
   Write a synonym for the following.

   a. better _____   b. within _____

   c. era _____   d. visible _____

3. Write the root for *preparation*. _____

E **Vowel Check.** Each of the following words needs an r-controlled vowel to complete it. Rewrite the word on the line provided. Be careful. Some words have two vowels missing.

1. ___ ___ din ___ y _____

2. sinc ___ ___ ___ _____

3. app ___ ___ _____

4. t ___ ___ rit ___ y _____

5. w ___ ___ y _____

6. ___ ___ selves _____

7. w ___ ___ ing _____

8. s ___ ___ ious _____

9. ___ ea _____

10. mat ___ ___ ial _____

11. prep ___ ___ ___ _____

12. int ___ ___ i ___ _____

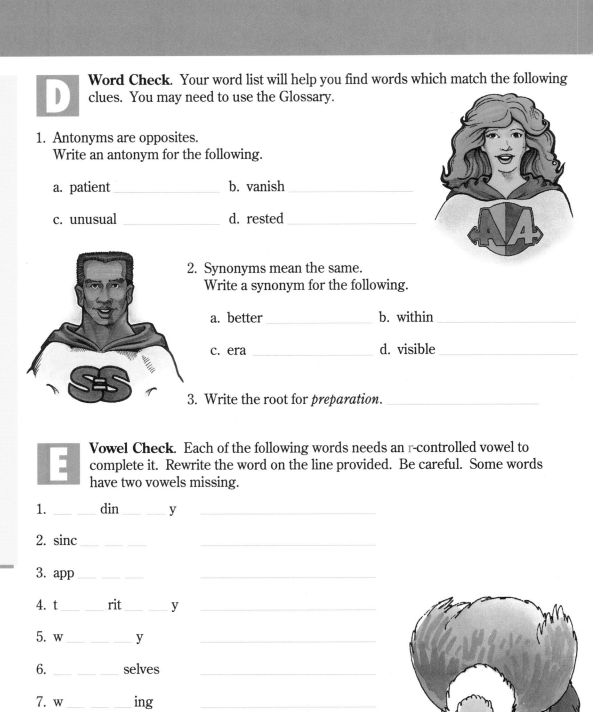

EXTERIOR

INTERIOR

F **Distant Friends.** Read the following letter.

Proofreading.

1. Insert commas in two places in the letter.
2. Proper nouns like *Ed, Bible,* and *Boston* should be capitalized. Find ten proper nouns and write them correctly in the space between the lines.
3. Underline at least twelve r-controlled vowel words in the letter. Rewrite these words in the margins of this page.

Dear tom

We arrived in july to begin our missionary work in argentina. The weather is often very cool because we are south of the equator and it is winter not summer. We are trying to get used to our different surroundings.

i met a boy named juan. That would be john in english. He seems very interested in the lord. He finds it hard to believe my family would give up our nice things to work with the people here.

Pray for me and my parents that we are able to share the gospel with patients at the clinic.

*Your friend
mike*

G **Dialogue Journal.**

1. Write a sentence about where missionaries live. _____

2. Have an older friend or relative respond to your sentence.

3. Now it's your turn again! Write a sentence telling something missionaries might do _____

4. Have your friend or relative respond again. _____

5. How would you feel about one day being a missionary yourself?

sincere
choices
calendars
grammar
continued
chapter
anyway
worst
prepare
destroy
produce
curved
orbit
normal
major
ordinary
prayer
therefore
regular
particular
daily
wearing
pursuit
loosen
apparent

A **Vowel Digraph Review.**

A vowel digraph is two _____ combined

to make their own _____ .

Write your words with the following digraphs.

oi spelled oi as in *oil* _____

oi spelled oy as in *joy* _____

ā spelled ai as in *aid* _____

ā spelled ay as in *day* _____

er as in *errand* spelled ayer _____

B **Review Long u and oo.**
1. Write your words with the following spellings for the long oo and u sounds.

spelled oo _____

spelled u _____

spelled ue _____

spelled u-e _____

spelled ui _____

Regular review *produces* rave results!

2. Find the word with two pronunciations. Write it with the correct accent mark for each definition.

to make something _____

vegetables and fruit _____

3. Write the word for which each abbreviation stands.

Ave. _____

Eur. _____

N. A. _____   Sun. _____

Dr. _____   St. _____

Mr. _____   Ps. _____

C **Review Spellings for Schwa + r**. Find the words with the following spellings for ər.

ər is spelled er _____

ər is spelled ar _____ _____

_____ _____

ər is spelled ur _____ _____

ər is spelled or _____ _____

What are you wearing tomorrow?

D **More R-Controlled Vowels**.

1. Find the words in which or says ȯr. _____

_____ _____ _____

2. Circle and rewrite the three words in which the wor says wər.

worst	worthy	wore	worship	worn

_____ _____ _____

3. Find the words with the following sounds.

Prepare the way of the Lord!

ir as in *here* _____

er as in *care* or *errand* _____ _____

_____ _____ _____

4. Find the words with the following descriptions.

having on the body _____ without hypocrisy _____

get ready _____ easily seen _____

E **Word Building**. Write the root word for the following.

destruction _____ irregularity _____

production _____ apparently _____

preparation _____ particularly _____

normally _____ ordinarily _____

orbital _____ sincerity _____

49

choices
anyway
destroy
prayer
daily
continued
produce
regular
pursuit
loosen
calendars
grammar
chapter
curved
particular
worst
orbit
normal
major
therefore
sincere
prepare
ordinary
wearing
apparent

F **Vowel Check**. Fill in the correct vowels plus r. Then write the word.

gramm _____ _____   calend _____ s _____

chapt _____ _____   p ____ ticul _____ _____

c ____ ved _____   w _____ ing _____

____ bit _____   _____ din ____ y _____

n ____ mal _____   th ____ f _____

maj _____ _____   sinc _____ _____

w ____ st _____   app ____ ent _____

prep _____ _____   pr _____ _____

p ____ suit _____   regul _____ _____

G **Classification**. Write a list word which completes the series.

1. lasted, endured, _____   5. section, episode, _____

2. career, interest, _____   6. certain, definite, _____

3. months, days, _____   7. visible, obvious, _____

4. usual, average, _____ or   8. truthful, genuine, _____

_____ or _____

H **Picture This**. Write the words which these clues indicate.

L⬭⬭SE   curved

_____   _____   _____

I **Grammar Check**.

1. Write two past tense words. _____ _____

2. Write two plurals. _____ _____

3. Write two compound words. _____ _____

J **Choices.** Life is full of choices, and a Christian should be careful to make wise ones.

1. Look up these verses and tell what to choose.

Deuteronomy 30:19 _____

Joshua 24:15 _____

Proverbs 16:16 _____ rather than _____

Proverbs 22:1 _____ rather than _____

and _____ rather than _____ and _____

2. Look up Proverbs 3:31 and tell what you should not choose. _____

_____

3. Look up the following verses and tell what was chosen.

Judges 5:8 and 10:14 _____

Job 36:21 _____

Psalm 119:30 _____

Psalm 119:173 _____

Hebrews 11:25 Moses chose to _____

_____ rather than _____

_____.

K **Word Find**. Find 17 of your list words in the following puzzle.

```
P  T  H  E  R  E  F  O  R  E  R
T  I  B  R  O  O  W  L  A  R  C
N  D  U  C  E  S  O  O  M  A  O
E  P  R  A  Y  E  R  O  M  P  N
R  R  O  J  A  M  S  S  A  E  T
A  I  C  H  A  P  T  E  R  R  I
P  N  W  E  A  R  I  N  G  P  N
P  U  R  S  U  I  T  C  E  R  U
A  N  Y  W  A  Y  E  R  E  G  E
D  A  I  L  Y  O  R  T  S  E  D
S  E  C  I  O  H  C  U  L  A  R
```

Beginning at the top left and going right, use the letters you did not circle to make three other words.

_____

_____

_____

Enter your scores for this lesson and your average for the six weeks on the graph in the back of your book.

parallel
million
average
forty-four
figure
remainder
mathematics
percent
solution
squares
ninth
geometry
solve
calculate
cubes
denominator
dividing
multiplying
estimate
fractions

A **Work With Your Words.** Which one of your list words is suggested by the following pictures? Write the list word on the line provided.

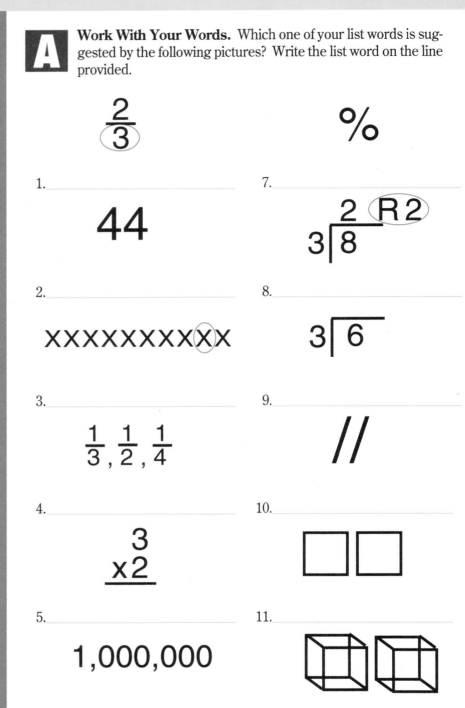

$\frac{2}{3}$

%

1. _____

7. _____

44

$3\overline{)8}$ 2 R 2

2. _____

8. _____

xxxxxxxxxx

$3\overline{)6}$

3. _____

9. _____

$\frac{1}{3}, \frac{1}{2}, \frac{1}{4}$

//

4. _____

10. _____

$\begin{array}{r} 3 \\ \times 2 \\ \hline \end{array}$

□ □

5. _____

11. _____

1,000,000

6. _____

12. _____

Choose several of your Home Base Words and draw a picture which will suggest each word. Have a friend write the words below the pictures you draw.

Then He took the five loaves and the two fish, ...and gave them to the multitude. So they all ate and were filled, and twelve baskets of the left-over fragments were taken up. (Luke 9:16-17)

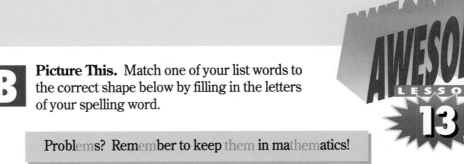
B **Picture This.** Match one of your list words to the correct shape below by filling in the letters of your spelling word.

Problems? Remember to keep them in mathematics!

1.

2.

3.

4.

5.

6.

7.

8.

C **Work With Numbers.**

1. Spell these numbers, each containing a form of *four*.

    40 _____   4 _____

    14 _____   4th _____

2. Spell these numbers, each containing a form of *nine*.

    90 _____   9 _____

    19 _____   9th _____

3. Spell these numbers, each giving an ordinal position.

    9th _____   20th _____

    10th _____   15th _____

4. Write these hyphenated numbers. For example, 21 is twenty-one.

    44 _____   31 _____

    72 _____   83 _____

5. Three of your list words mean to compute or to find the answer to a problem. Find them and write them below.

    _____ _____ _____

6. a. Which of your list words is a number found by adding several digits and then dividing by the number of digits? b. Which is a number you get by making a guess based on facts?

    a. _____   b. _____

53

D **Name the Category.** Look at each group of words and figure out how they are related. Choose one of your list words which would make a good title for the group. In some groups, you will add a word from your list which also fits in the group.

Word List:
parallel
million
average
forty-four
figure
remainder
mathematics
percent
solution
squares
ninth
geometry
solve
calculate
cubes
denominator
dividing
multiplying
estimate
fractions

1. mixed number
   numerator

   _____

   TITLE: _____

2. factors
   product
   multiplicand

   TITLE: _____

3. fourth
   sixth
   seventh

   _____

   TITLE: **order**

4. quadrillion
   trillion

   _____

   TITLE: **large numbers**

5. lines
   rectangles

   _____

   _____

   TITLE: _____

6. dividend
   divisor
   quotient

   _____

   TITLE: _____

7. algebra
   calculus
   trigonometry

   _____

   TITLE: _____

Remember that some words must be "fixed" before you can add a suffix. Words that end in y keep the y when adding ing to the root. For example, *fly + ing = flying*. But words that end in e drop the e to add ing. For example, *write + ing = writing*.

E **Work With Suffixes.** Add ing to the following words.

1. carry + ing = _____
2. solve + ing = _____
3. buy + ing = _____
4. estimate + ing = _____
5. multiply + ing = _____
6. divide + ing = _____
7. supply + ing = _____
8. figure + ing = _____
9. bury + ing = _____
10. calculate + ing = _____

F **Hink Pinks**. A *hink pink* is a two-word phrase that rhymes, like *hink* and *pink*. Look at the descriptions below. Find a list word that fits part of the clue; then add a rhyming word that answers the description. Write the two-word phrase on the line. For example: *An unhappy boy* would be a *sad lad.*

1. an answer to the problem of litter and smog _____

2. hollow containers for six-sided figures _____

3. things done with numbers having a numerator and denominator _____

4. four-sided figures belonging to rabbits _____

5. a larger symbol for a number _____

G **Story Completion.** Read the following story. Fill in the blanks with list words or forms of list words. The shapes can be filled in with words of your choice. The story is based on Luke 9:11-17.

Multitudes followed Jesus to a deserted place. Jesus spoke to them and healed many who were _____. When it got late, the _____ thought to send them away so they could get something to ⟨fish⟩. Jesus told the disciples to ⟨fish⟩ them. The disciples could _____ there were about 5,000 men; so they knew the little boy's five _____ and ⟨fish⟩ fish would not be enough. Jesus had a _____ to the problem. He had the _____ sit in groups, then gave _____ for the food. The _____ handed out the small amount of ⟨fish⟩, and all were fed. They collected the _____ and had twelve _____ full! Jesus had _____ the food by _____ it among the people.

H **Dialogue Journal Writing.** Use a piece of paper or a notebook. Answer each question in a complete sentence. Then have someone else respond to your answer before going on to the next question.

1. Why do you think Jesus performed this miracle?
2. How do you think the little boy felt after Jesus used his bread and fish?
3. Tell about another of Jesus' miracles that you especially like. Tell why you like it.

common
command
conduct
contract
complete
collection
combine
comment*
accustom
diamond
connection
lovingly
others
discovery
doves
anonymous*
covenant
smother
considerate
concerned

A **Background.** All of this week's words have an o followed by m, n, l, v, or th. This o usually makes a short u or the schwa sound unless it is in an accented syllable. Place your words below according to their spellings. One of your words will go in two places.

1. Place all the om words on the computer.
2. Place all the ol words on the cologne.
3. Place all the on words on the money.
4. Place all the ov words on the glove.
5. Place all the oth words on Mother Goose.

6. Put a star by two words on the computer which are accented on the first syllable. Notice the short o sound.
7. Put a star by a word on the money which has four syllables and is accented on the second syllable. Notice the short o sound.
8. Add any of your Home Base Words which have a schwa o sound to the correct pictures.

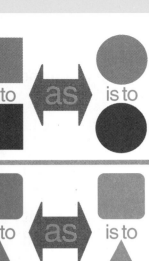

B **Analogies.** Complete each of the following analogies with one of your list words.

1. Roughly is to gently as spitefully is to

_____ .

2. Ravens are to crows as _____ are to pigeons.

3. Scientist is to invention as explorer is to _____ .

4. Tennis is to court as baseball is to _____ .

5. Players are to team as stamps are to _____ .

6. Ill-mannered is to rude as polite is to _____ .

C **Double Saying.** Three of your words have two pronunciations. Both pronunciations are used in each of these sentences. Decide which pronunciation goes in which blank and write the word with the accent mark in the correct place. Use the Glossary if you need help.

1. If we _____ our efforts and use the _____ , we will finish the harvest sooner. (com′ bine, com bine′)

2. If you _____ yourself better this quarter, you will earn a better mark in

_____ . (con′ duct, con duct′)

3. If we get the _____ , our lab people will see if the new material will

_____ . (con′ tract, con tract′)

D **Short Definitions.** Find a list word to match each of the following definitions. Use your Glossary if you need help.

1. get used to

_____

2. everyone else

_____

3. a joining together

_____

4. suffocate

_____

5. things gathered together

_____

6. mix together

_____

7. give orders

_____

8. tenderly

_____

9. burdened

_____

Don't forget to add your Home Base Words to your Glossary.

E **Go for Third.** In each of the following sets of words, the first two are related in some way. Look at them carefully and decide how they are related. Then find one of your list words which is related in the same way.

1. robins, sparrows,

5. pen name, unknown,

2. lead, guide,

6. remark, statement,

3. ruby, emerald,

7. finished, whole,

4. ordinary, usual,

8. contract, promise,

F **Alterations.** Exchange the prefix in each of the following words with another prefix to make one of your list words.

1. demand   ⟶

2. discerned   ⟶

3. distract   ⟶

4. recovery   ⟶

5. deplete   ⟶

6. selection   ⟶

G **Labels.** Write one of your list words beneath each of the following pictures.

Use two of these words in sentences.

---

common
command
conduct
contract
complete
collection
combine
comment
accustom
diamond
connection
lovingly
others
discovery
doves
anonymous
covenant
smother
considerate
concerned

H **Alphabetical Order.** Many of your words begin with the letter c. See if you can accurately place them in alphabetical order below. Be careful: Sometimes you will have to look at the fifth letter to get them in correct order!

1. collection

2. _____

3. _____

4. _____

5. common

6. _____

7. _____

8. _____

9. connection

10. _____

11. _____

12. _____

I **Did You Know?** A *covenant* is a promise, usually between two people or groups of people. Both parties are obligated to fulfill their part of the promise or the covenant is no longer effective. God's covenants are wonderful because He will always do His part. He promised Abraham He would give him a land. God promised Israel that He would establish them as His people. God promised David that He would establish his kingdom forever. Though several of God's covenants have not yet been fulfilled, they have only been postponed until Christ returns.

Your descendants will be more numerous than the stars.

J **Write About It.** God has many promises in Scripture. Some of them concern our salvation, some of them concern answered prayer, and some give promise of other special blessings. Think of a promise you particularly like. Tell what is promised and why you especially like it. Also, tell if there is anything you are obligated to do to receive the promise. If you need some help, you may want to start with Psalm 37. Use your Word Bank for spelling assistance.

_____

_____

_____

_____

_____

_____

_____

_____

general
central
metal
local
bugle
practical
bundle
evil
musical
medal
icicle
tabernacle
valuable
devil
angels
angles
troublesome
meddle
freckles
assemble

A **Work With Your Words.** All of this week's words have a schwa l sound at the end of the root word. This sound is spelled el, le, al, or il. Group your words below according to the schwa plus l spelling.

al as in *normal*   le as in *buckle*

il as in *pencil*

el as in *panel*

Draw lines in the correct places above and add any Home Base Words which have a schwa plus l sound. Also place them in your Word Bank.

B **A Look At Your Words.** Look for the following in your word list.

1. Three plurals

2. A compound

3. Two words with double consonants. Divide them into syllables, using the Glossary if needed.

C
Clues. Use the following clues to identify words from your word list.

1. This le is frozen. _____

2. These les have degrees. _____

3. These les come out in the sun. _____

4. This le is expensive. _____

5. This le is a tent. _____

6. This le awakens you at camp. _____

7. This le doesn't mind its own business. _____

8. This le is a bunch. _____

9. This le is full of problems. _____

10. This al is in the middle. _____

11. This al uses good sense. _____

12. This al has authority. _____

13. This al comes from the neighborhood. _____

14. This al is worn proudly. _____

15. This al could be gold or silver. _____

16. This al might use the piano. _____

Multiple freckles: A practical, non-troublesome tan!

D
Homophones. *Medal* and *meddle* sound alike, but have different meanings. *Metal* also sounds like *medal*. Look up all three in the Glossary, write a short definition in the box, and use them correctly in the following sentences.

| medal = _____ |
| metal = _____ |
| meddle = _____ |

1. He received a _____ at the banquet.

2. If it isn't your problem, don't _____.

3. Our bookcase is made of _____.

4. The _____ he won is in the cabinet.

5. Gold is a valuable _____.

6. If you _____, you may destroy a friendship.

Don't *meddle* with the *metal medals*!

Picture This. Look at each picture, trace over the letters in each word picture, then write the word.

1.

2.

3.

4.

5.

6. me le

7.

1. _____

2. _____

3. _____

4. _____

5. _____

6. _____

7. _____

8. What word do you see in *devil* which will help you remember its spelling?

_____

Acrostic. Fill in the acrostic below, using one of your words for each clue. The letters in the boxes going down will spell a word which means having worth.

1. _____

2. _____

3. _____

4. _____

5. _____

6. _____

7. _____

8. _____

The letters in the boxes going down spell _____, which means having worth.

Word list:

general
central
metal
local
bugle
practical
bundle
evil
musical
medal
icicle
tabernacle
valuable
devil
angels
angles
troublesome
meddle
freckles
assemble

Clues:

1. one of Satan's names
2. near the center
3. wicked
4. a bunch
5. useful, sensible
6. to gather
7. bothersome
8. common, for all

Unto you is born this day a Savior! Jesus!

G **Did You Know?** *Angels* are heavenly beings who were created by God and are a little higher than man. There is a vast multitude of them. They assist, protect, deliver, and sometimes guide God's people. They have appeared to people in bodily form. In the Old Testament, the Angel of the Lord is believed to be Christ, a foreshadow of His coming in the flesh.

H **Write About It.** You are an angel. Or, let's just pretend you are! You are going to appear to one of the great Bible characters, or one of the not-so-great Bible characters. There are many to choose from—Samson's parents, John the Baptist's parents, Mary, Joseph, the shepherds, Jesus, Daniel, Philip, Paul, Balaam, Sarai, Elijah, and many more. Decide to whom you will appear, why you are appearing, and what you will say. You may also want to describe how you look. Write about it below.

_____

_____

_____

_____

_____

_____

Remember that g before e has a soft sound (*angel*), and g before a consonant has a hard sound (*angle*).

I **Angels or Angles?** *Angel* and *angle* are often confused. Look them up in the Glossary, and use them or their plural form in the sentences below.

1. An _____ appeared to Mary.

2. How many degrees are in this _____ ?

3. A right _____ has ninety degrees.

4. We need three people to be _____ in the program.

5. The _____ announced Christ's birth to the shepherds.

6. We will measure all the _____ with a protractor.

Be sure to record scores.

advice
advisable
advisory
revise
revision
supervisor
televise
televisions
video tape
visible
visibility
visitors
visors
visual
convertible
reverse
universe
university
conversed
verb
verbal
verses
version
revival
revive
survival
vital
vitality
vitamins
vivid

Base Words. This week's words are built on four Latin root words. Check the list and write the root next to the meaning. Check the Glossary if you need help.

vis	vers	vit	vert

1. _____ to have life

2. _____ to see, look

3. _____ words

4. _____ to change

Each of these roots has alternate spellings. Check your list and write a second spelling for each root. Then write the meaning of the root underneath.

1. vit → _____

3. vers → _____

2. vis → _____

4. vert → _____

Locate 18 of your list words in this Word Find.

```
V  I  T  A  L  I  T  Y  S  R  O  S  I  V
E  S  I  V  E  L  E  T  E  C  I  V  D  A
S  R  E  I  A  D  V  I  S  A  B  L  E  V
R  O  L  D  I  V  E  S  R  D  I  V  I  V
E  T  B  E  V  L  S  R  E  V  I  V  A  L
V  I  I  O  A  B  R  E  V  I  S  E  N  U
E  S  S  T  E  L  E  V  I  S  I  O  N  S
R  I  I  A  I  V  V  I  N  S  B  R  E  V
E  V  V  P  R  E  I  N  U  E  I  V  E  R
V  I  V  E  S  R  S  U  R  V  I  V  A  L
```

B **Syllable Sense.** Check your list words for syllables and write them correctly in the forms below. Trace the letters that have been written for you.

vis

verse

vit

ver

vi

vis

vice

vid

vi

vise

ver

viv

vi

ver

viv

vive

vi

vert

vi

vis

verse

vis

versed

 C **Parts of Speech.** Write in list words to make the changes below; then write a sentence using the word. The first one is done for you.

1. advise (verb) ⟶ advice (noun/thing)

   Coach Davis gave me good advice.

2. supervise (verb) ⟶ _____ (noun/person)

   _____

3. _____ (verb) ⟶ conversation (noun/thing)

   _____

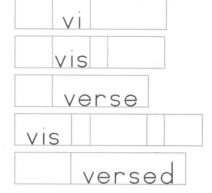

Suffixes often change the use of a word in a sentence. For example, a change in suffix may change the word from a verb to a noun or adjective.

4. revive (verb) ⟶ _____ (noun/thing)

   _____

5. _____ (adjective) ⟶ vitality (noun/thing)

   _____

6. televise (verb) ⟶ _____ (noun/thing)

   _____

7. convert (verb) ⟶ _____ (noun/thing)

   _____

advice
advisable
advisory
revise
revision
supervisor
televise
televisions
video tape
visible
visibility
visitors
visors
visual
convertible
reverse
universe
university
conversed
verb
verbal
verses
version
revival
revive
survival
vital
vitality
vitamins
vivid

D **Working With Prefixes.** Combine a prefix with each given root and write the new word next to the given meaning.

1. *vis*

_____ to oversee

_____ to send a far distance to be seen

_____ to look at your paragraph again and make any changes needed

2. *vers*

_____ talked with

3. *vert*

_____ to change back again

_____ all of creation

4. *viv*

_____ to bring to life again

_____ overcoming a dangerous threat

| ad = to | tele = far | re = again |
| con = with | uni = one |
| super,sur = over |

E **A Hospital Visit.** Complete each sentence using a list word.

1. Marie was happy to have _____ (people) come to see her in the hospital.

2. The nurse said it was _____ (ideal) to stay only a few minutes.

3. Although she had surgery, her scars were not very _____ (observable).

4. We _____ (talked) with her only a short while.

5. Pastor Carter then read some _____ (Scripture) from Romans 8.

6. When we were ready to leave, we thanked God for her _____ (continuing to live) after such a bad accident.

F **Categorical Cases.** The two words listed give clues to a category. Complete each group with a list word.

1. noun, adjective, _____

2. planets, world, _____

3. sports coupe, station wagon, _____

4. telegraphs, telephones, _____

5. minerals, calories, _____

6. books, chapters, _____

7. change, alter, _____

8. important, essential, _____

9. school, college, _____

10. talked, spoke, _____

11. lively, colorful, _____

12. sunglasses, hats, _____

13. recommendation, counsel, _____

14. filmstrip, movie, _____

G **Did You Know?** *Revive* means to give life back. The psalmist prayed, "Will you not revive us (your people)?" (Psalm 85:6) In the history of the church, many great revivals have swept through whole countries, bringing a sorrow for sin and a new dedication to the work of God. Mighty revivals have always begun with Christians praying.

H **Write About It.** Write a prayer to the Lord for revival in your church, school, home, or in your own heart.

Dear Lord, _____

_____

_____

_____

_____

_____

_____

_____

_____

oceans
forests
citizens
population
continents
equator
environment
atmosphere
regions
international
transportation
conservation
resources
arctic
pollution
liter
passports
preserving
global
litter

A

Work With Your Words. Find one of your words which describes an area of the globe below. Fill in the name which matches the number on the globe.

1   3

2   4

1. _____   3. _____

2. _____   4. _____

B

Which Fits? Look up *international* and *global* in the Glossary. Decide which word fits best in each sentence below.

1. World War II was a _____ war.

2. The _____ conference involving China, Japan, and the U.S. is being held in Tokyo.

Look up *population* and *citizens* in the Glossary. Decide which word fits best in each sentence below.

1. The census showed our _____ to be about two million.

2. As _____, you should exercise your right to vote.

C

Plurals. Write all of your words which are plurals.

_____   _____

_____   _____

_____   _____

_____

Usually, plurals are made by adding _____ or _____ to the root word.

D   **Conservation.** Fill in each blank below with one of your words.

Many people are concerned about what is happening to our world. Both scientists and

ordinary _____ want to protect our _____. They see many of our

natural _____ being wasted, resources which cannot easily be restored. For example, many of

our national_____ are disappearing as careless people start fires or land is cleared for new projects.

Our _____ is in danger as well. _____ results

when industries send wastes into the air. Our rivers, streams, and

_____ also become polluted as tons of

_____ are dumped into them.

Many people have formed groups to make us more aware of what is

happening to our world. These _____

groups work to pass and enforce laws. They are responsible for

_____ some of our land areas by making them

national parks.

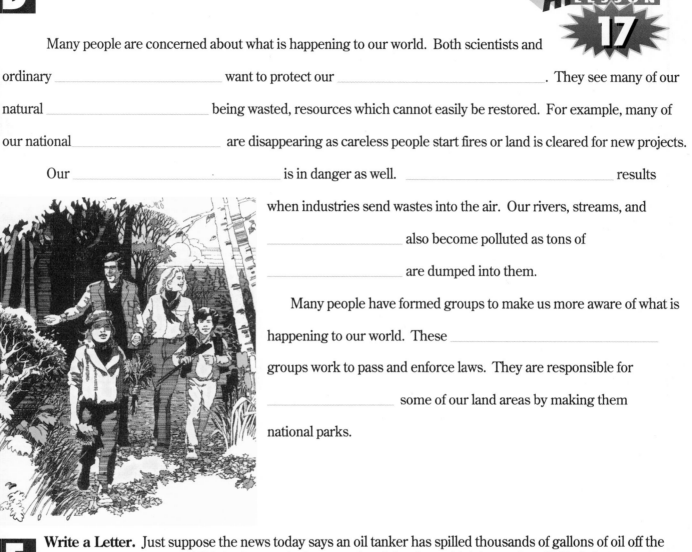

E   **Write a Letter.** Just suppose the news today says an oil tanker has spilled thousands of gallons of oil off the coast of your country. Wildlife in the area is threatened and the river which is nearby will likely become contaminated. That means the water of several cities in the area is also in danger of being polluted. Write a letter to the Governor or President telling how you feel as a citizen who is concerned about the future of your country.

_____

_____

_____

_____

_____

Be sure your Home Base Words and scores have been recorded.

oceans
forests
citizens
population
continents
equator
environment
atmosphere
regions
international
transportation
conservation
resources
arctic
pollution
liter
passports
preserving
global
litter

F **Metric and English Measures.** In the United States, English measures are used, such as quarts, miles and ounces. However, many other nations use the metric system, involving liters, kilometers and grams. Some countries spell *liter* as *litre* and *meter* as *metre*. Use the pictures to help you fill in the equivalents below.

English		Metric
1. 1 quart	=	.95 _____
2. 1 gallon	=	3.79 _____
3. 1 _____	=	2.54 centimeters
4. 1 _____	=	.91 meters
5. 1 mile	=	1.61 _____
6. 1 ounce	=	28.3 _____
7. 1 _____	=	.45 kilograms

BOSTON
1 mile
(1.61 km.)

1 yard

inch

1 meter

cm cm cm

G **Glossary Glimpse.** Look up the following words in your Glossary and place the accent mark where it belongs. Then rewrite the word. Do three of your Home Base Words for numbers 8 - 10.

1. lit ter _____

2. arc tic _____

3. pass ports _____

4. re gions _____

5. li ter _____

6. trans por ta tion _____

7. glo bal _____

8. _____

9. _____

10. _____

The Glossary can be your guide to locate the accent mark in words. The accent mark tells which syllable gets a stronger emphasis when it is pronounced.

H **Litter Vs. Liter.** Don't confuse *litter* with *liter*. Look up the words in the Glossary and fill in the following sentences correctly with a form of *litter* or *liter*.

1. There is a fine for _____ along the highway.

2. We bought a _____ bottle of soda.

70

Combinations. Many of this week's words come from a foreign root and prefix. Study the information in the box; then decide which of your words fits the literal definition below.

prefix	meaning
con	together
en	within
inter	among
pol	throughout
pre	before
re	again
trans	across

root	meaning
atmos	vapor
equate	make equal
viron	area
populus	people
port	carry
serve	guard
source	origin
sphere	round
tin	hold

1. vapor around

2. guarding together

3. land held together

4. within an area

5. that which makes equal

6. among nations

7. group of people

8. guarding before

9. original things to use again

10. carrying across

Responsibility. *Responsibility* is doing what God expects you to do. God has given us some responsibilities in relation to His creation. The Bible says man has dominion over God's creation. Dominion means power or authority to rule over. Read the following Scriptures and tell what specific things man has the responsibility to rule.

1. Genesis 1:26

2. Daniel 2:38

3. Hebrews 2:7

Christians are responsible to be good stewards of the earth.

parallel
million
squares
mathematics
ninth
common
collection
accustom
lovingly
others
central
practical
evil
valuable
angels
advice
supervisor
convertible
verses
vital
oceans
forests
citizens
environment
arctic

A **Successful Math.**

1. Match one of your words with each of the following clues.

shapes _____   after eight others _____

large number _____   describes lines _____

a subject in school _____

2. Spell the following number words.

4 _____   9 _____

4th _____   9th _____

14 _____   19 _____

44 _____   99 _____

3. Check Lesson 13 for words suggested by these pictures.

$$1/4, 1/3, 1/2$$

$$4\overline{)14} \quad \dfrac{3}{} \; \textbf{R2}$$

_____

% _____

$$5/6$$ _____

4. Add ing to the following words.

calculate _____   divide _____

multiply _____   figure _____

subtract _____   borrow _____

estimate _____   add _____

average _____   solve _____

Words that end in _____ keep the _____ when adding ing.
Words that end in _____ drop the _____ to add ing.

B Review Schwa O.

1. When o is followed by m, n, l, v, or th, the o often has a short u or schwa sound. Find a list word which has the following spellings. Then write another form of the word by adding a different prefix or suffix.

əm spelled om _____   _____

əl spelled ol _____   _____

əv spelled ov _____   _____

ən spelled on _____   _____

əth spelled oth _____   _____

2. Find a word which completes each phrase. Check Lesson 14 for help.

a. captain gave a _____

b. _____ the picture

c. a scientific _____

d. signed a _____

e. two carat _____

f. _____ phone call

C Review Schwa + L.

1. Find the əl sound with the following spellings:

il _____   al _____

le _____   al _____

el _____

Reviewing is a *valuable*, *practical* way to build word power!

2. Use *medal*, *meddle*, or *metal* correctly in the following sentences:

Don't _____ in the affairs of others.

Use a special paint so the _____ won't rust.

He received a _____ for first place.

3. Use *angle* and *angel* correctly in the following sentences:

An _____ of the Lord delivered the message.

An acute _____ has less than ninety degrees.

parallel
million
squares
mathematics
ninth
common
collection
accustom
lovingly
others
central
practical
evil
valuable
angels
advice
supervisor
convertible
verses
vital
oceans
forests
citizens
environment
arctic

D **Word Building.**

1. Find list words with the following roots:

   vis meaning to see _____ _____

   vit meaning to have life _____

   vers meaning words _____

   vert meaning to change _____

2. Write words with the following prefixes:

   ad meaning to _____

   con meaning with _____

   super meaning over _____

3. Each spectacle has a word in it. Move the related words from the word box to the correct spectacle.

visual   **vitality**

conversed
survival
university
reverse
televise
version
revise
universe
visible
revival
verb
vitamins

verbal   **convert**

4. Use *advice* and *advise* correctly in the following sentences:

   The doctor will usually give sound _____

   He will _____ you to get plenty of rest.

74

Revisiting Our World.

1. Match list words with the following clues.

cold _____   people _____

trees _____   water _____

surroundings _____

2. Put the correct labels on the following pictures. Use *kilometers*, *grams*, and *liters*.

COOL COLA 2   NEXT EXIT 3   CRISPY CHIPS 198

> Your dad's *convertible* sure has been handy since my hair dryer broke!

F **Clues.** Use the following clues to identify words from the word list:

This le is nice to ride in. _____

This le is priceless. _____

This al is important to life. _____

This al makes sensible choices. _____

This al is in the middle. _____

This el is made of lines. _____

G **Syllables.** Divide the following words into syllables. Rewrite the word on the line, drawing a line between the syllables. Use your Glossary, if needed.

million _____   collection _____

common _____   accustom _____

central _____   environment _____

angels _____   verses _____

advice _____   arctic _____

H **Write About It.** Choose one of the following titles and write a short essay. Check your Word Bank for spelling assistance. Proofread and correct your work. Rewrite your final copy.

Practical Advice   Citizens and the Environment   Millions of Angels   My Valuable Collection

Compute and enter your scores for this lesson and for the six weeks on your graph.

decision
position
condition
conversation
expression
description
selection
correction
mission
suggestion
vision
notion
session
foundation
provision
confession
compassion
introduction
comprehension
rotation

Work With Your Words. All of this week's words end in tion or sion. This ending usually says shən, but it can also say zhən or chən. Group your words below according to the spelling and pronunciation of the ending. Draw lines and place your Home Base Words where they belong.

tion says shən, as in *salvation*

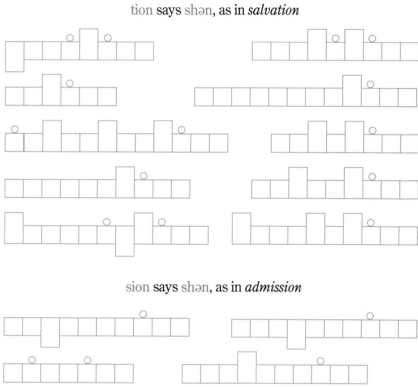

sion says shən, as in *admission*

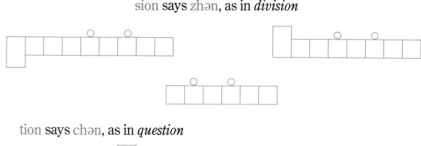

sion says zhən, as in *division*

tion says chən, as in *question*

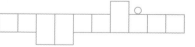

sion says chən, as in *apprehension*

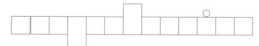

Be sure to add the Home Base Words to the Glossary.

B **Limerick.** In a limerick, the first, second, and fifth lines rhyme with each other. The third and fourth lines also rhyme. Fill in the following limerick with words from your list. Clues are in the box.

There once was a man with a _____. (1)

He saw the whole world as a _____. (2)
    He took off one day
    For the coasts of Bombay.

He had made an important _____. (3)

He knew the world's sinful _____, (4)

Which could only be changed by _____.(5)
    He preached Jesus Christ
    And His great gift of life.

So he won many souls with _____. (6)

1. dream
2. a work for missionaries
3. conclusion
4. state of health
5. admission of sin
6. sympathy

C **Roots.** Many of this week's words are the result of a suffix being added to a root word. Tell which of your words comes from each of these roots.

1. converse _____
2. correct _____

3. describe _____
4. decide _____

5. confess _____
6. suggest _____

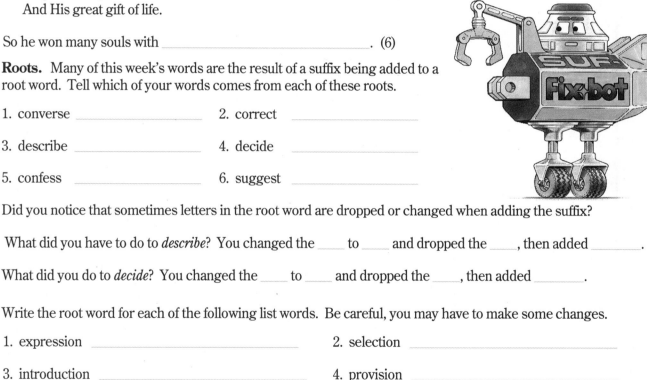

Did you notice that sometimes letters in the root word are dropped or changed when adding the suffix?

What did you have to do to *describe*? You changed the ____ to ____ and dropped the ____, then added _____.

What did you do to *decide*? You changed the ____ to ____ and dropped the ____, then added _____.

Write the root word for each of the following list words. Be careful, you may have to make some changes.

1. expression _____
2. selection _____

3. introduction _____
4. provision _____

5. comprehension _____
6. rotation _____

D **Did You Know?** *Conversation* in the Bible often refers to our conduct. Several New Testament references caution us to watch our *conversation*. These refer not only to our talking, but to our total behavior. When we become Christians, we are to put off all our former *conversation* (lifestyle) and be renewed in the Spirit (Eph. 5:22-23). As other people watch us and listen to us, they will know whether or not we are Christians.

Don't just talk the talk...but walk the walk!

decision
position
condition
conversation
expression
description
selection
correction
mission
suggestion
vision
notion
session
foundation
provision
confession
compassion
introduction
comprehension
rotation

Syllables. Dividing your words into syllables may help you in learning to spell this week's words. Write the following words and divide them into syllables by writing them into the boxes where the division occurs. Use your Glossary, if needed.

1. comprehension

2. condition

3. correction

4. foundation

5. notion

6. position

7. session

8. suggestion

F **Picture This.**

Remember that ti, si, ci, and xi can say sh, ch, or zh.

1. Means sight.

   Write it. _____

2. Means a spinning motion; a revolution.

   Write it. _____

3. Means the way something is placed, like how you sit. In fact, the word *sit* is in it.

   Write it. _____

4. Means the look on your face.

   Write it. _____

G **More News From Argentina.** Read the following letter.

Dear Tom,

It was great to get your letter I received it just the other day, but I noticed you had mailed it in November.

My family has been very busy since we arrived it took us a week to go buy supplies. we are fortunate to have a car Thank God for His provision.

Our mission is to see many people come to know Christ. in fact, we often have a conversation about how to be more effective. how can we be more available? Or, how can we show more compassion Father has built a good foundation for ministry at the clinic. we want to restore physical health, then we can bring spiritual health

the people here need the Savior. We have a challenging task

Your friend,
Mike

Help Mike proofread his letter.

1. The first word of every sentence should begin with a capital letter. Find six words that should have been capitalized and circle them in the letter.

2. Every sentence should end with punctuation. Put an exclamation point after the one sentence that shows excitement. Put a question mark after the one sentence that asks a question. Put a period after the four sentences that should have ended in a period.

3. Find five words that end with tion or sion. Check their spelling and write them below.

_____

_____

_____

_____

_____

H **Dialogue Journal.**

1. If you were Mike, what kind of things would you do to show compassion for the people of Argentina?

_____

2. Give this letter to someone else so he or she can respond to the question above and to your answer.

_____

3. Why do you think a clinic might be helpful in winning souls for Christ?

_____

4. Have someone else respond to question three and your answer.

_____

Continue your written conversation on other paper if you like.

future
furniture
century
appreciate
social
creature
precious
commercial
manufacture
associate
issue
substantial
parachute
politician
beneficial
glacier
measuring
reassure
treasury
sugary

A **Work With Your Words.** All of this week's words have an i or u following a consonant. This pattern can cause the pronunciation of the consonant to change. Group your words below according to the spelling and pronunciation of the consonant plus i or u.

c before i says sh as in *special*

t before u says ch as in *capture*

s before u says zh as in *pleasure*

s before u says sh as in *sure*

ch before u says sh as in *chute*

t before i says ch as in *question*

Add lines in the margins and write your Home Base Words that fit the patterns.

Naturally, it would *surely* make things more *efficient* if you would send your *treasury* of *essential* laundry down the *chute*.

How is the sh sound spelled in this lesson?

_____ i, _____ u, or _____ u

How is the ch sound spelled in this lesson? _____ u and _____ i

How is the zh sound spelled in this lesson? _____ u

B | **Picture This.** Match one of your spelling words to its correct shape.

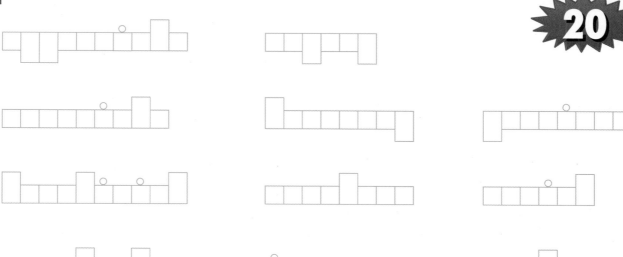

Make forms like those above for two of your Home Base Words.

Go back and write over the printed words in cursive with your favorite color. Choose another color and outline each configuration box twice.

Parts of my speech today will include nouns, verbs and adjectives.

C | **Parts of Speech.** The phrase "part of speech" refers to how a word is used in a sentence. Identify the words in the box below with the correct part of speech. Some words can go in two places. Use your Glossary if needed.

century	appreciate	social
manufacture	associate	substantial
beneficial	reassure	sugary
	glacier	

Noun   Verb   Adjective

_____   _____   _____

_____   _____   _____

_____   _____   _____

future
furniture
century
appreciate
social
creature
precious
commercial
manufacture
associate
issue
substantial
parachute
politician
beneficial
glacier
measuring
reassure
treasury
sugary

D **Contrasts.** To contrast is to point out a difference. Find a word from your list which completes the contrast in each phrase below. For example: not hard, but easy.

1. not harmful, but _____

2. not past, but _____

3. not to complain, but to _____

4. not salty, but _____

5. not a millennium, but a _____

6. not residential, but _____

E **Related Meanings.**

1. In Lesson 10, you learned that a *factor* originally was a doer or maker. A *factory* is a place where something is made. So, to _____ is to make by hand or with machinery.

2. _____ means to *assure* again, or give confidence to.

3. To *furnish* a home, you must have _____ .

4. A *created* being is a _____ .

5. Using a ruler or *meter*stick, you could be _____ for new curtains.

6. A nation's money (*treasure*) is handled by a _____ department.

The *manufacturer* of this *parachute* *reassured* me that it's good to the very last drop! I *appreciate* it, too!

F **Did You Know?** The idea of using a *parachute* goes back to at least 1515 when Leonardo da Vinci drew a picture of a cloth parachute in the shape of a pyramid. Two novels, published in 1595 and 1632, have main characters who used parachutes to jump from buildings. The first successful parachute jump was made in 1783 when Sebastien Lenormand jumped from a tower. In 1797, Andre Jacques Garnerin went up in a hot-air balloon, cut the cords which held his parachute to the balloon, and came down 3,000 feet safely. The first nylon parachute was produced in 1939.

G **For Your Information.** The word *sugar* comes from the ancient Indian word *sakara* which meant sand or gravel. It became *sukkar* in Arabic, *sucre* in French, *azúcar* in Spanish, and *sugar* in English.

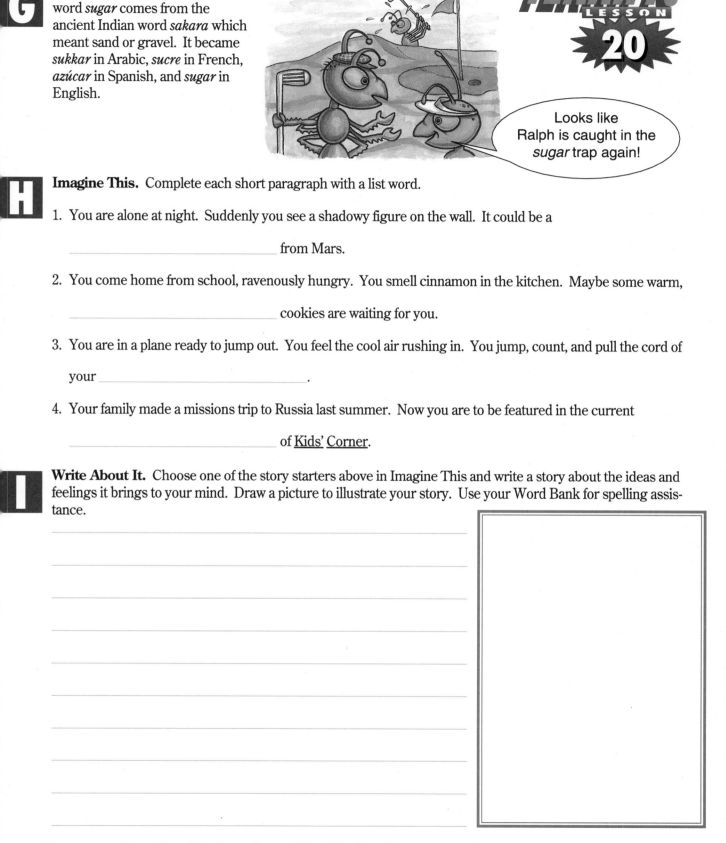

Looks like Ralph is caught in the *sugar* trap again!

H **Imagine This.** Complete each short paragraph with a list word.

1. You are alone at night. Suddenly you see a shadowy figure on the wall. It could be a

   _____ from Mars.

2. You come home from school, ravenously hungry. You smell cinnamon in the kitchen. Maybe some warm,

   _____ cookies are waiting for you.

3. You are in a plane ready to jump out. You feel the cool air rushing in. You jump, count, and pull the cord of

   your _____ .

4. Your family made a missions trip to Russia last summer. Now you are to be featured in the current

   _____ of <u>Kids' Corner</u>.

I **Write About It.** Choose one of the story starters above in Imagine This and write a story about the ideas and feelings it brings to your mind. Draw a picture to illustrate your story. Use your Word Bank for spelling assistance.

_____

_____

_____

_____

_____

_____

_____

_____

_____

_____

Be sure your Home Base Words are in your Word Bank and that your scores are recorded on your graph.

affect
affection
defect
defector
effect
effective
imperfection
perfection
perfectly
confusion
defuse
diffuse
fusion
refuse
refusing
transfusion
contradict
dictate
dictator
dictionaries
edict
predict
prediction
deportation
exported
imports
reporting
transport
transportable
transporting

A **Base Words.** This week's list words are built on four roots. These are fect, fuse, dict, and port. Study your words and write the root above its meaning.

1. _____
to carry or move across

2. _____
to do throughout to completion

3. _____
to blend together, mix

4. _____
to speak out clearly

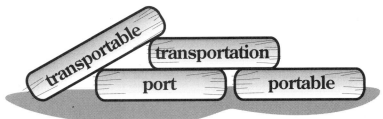

B **Affect vs. Effect.** Like the words *accept* and *except*, the use of *affect* and *effect* can be confusing. It helps to remember that *affect* is related to our feelings. For example, *affection* means love. The meaning to remember is "to influence."

Effect means result in. As a verb, it is a forceful word meaning to work to cause something to happen or change. Because we cannot force others to change, we use the word *affect* (influence) most of the time. Occasionally we use *effect* when we really mean that we made a change happen.

Choose the correct word in parentheses to complete each sentence.

1. The rainy weather _____ (affected, effected) our mood.

2. Beautiful music _____ (affects, effects) the way we worship.

3. Mr. Keenan _____ (affected, effected) a change in our lunchroom system.

4. The medicine Dr. Simpson prescribed was very _____ . (effective, affecting)

5. Terry is very _____ (effective, affectionate) with her parents.

C Typing Tokens.

Doug's computer types parts of words, but he hit the shift bar and typed numbers instead. Help him out by writing the words he meant to type. Remember to make the necessary spelling changes when combining parts of words.

8, 10, 11	6, 16, 18	15, 2, 3
13, 6, 3	15, 7, 3	1, 10, 9
15, 2, 18	12, 10, 14	5, 2, 3
1, 7, 3	6, 3, 4, 14	1, 10, 11
12, 5, 2, 3	15, 10, 16, 3	8, 7, 11

D Parts of Speech. Complete the chart using list words.

Verb	Another verb form	Noun form	Adjective form
	defected		defective
	dictating		dictatorial
		transportation	
		refusal	
	predicted		predictable
	affected		

affect
affection
defect
defector
effect
effective
imperfection
perfection
perfectly
confusion
defuse
diffuse
fusion
refuse
refusing
transfusion
contradict
dictate
dictator
dictionaries
edict
predict
prediction
deportation
exported
imports
reporting
transport
transportable
transporting

E **Working With Meanings.** Check your Glossary for definitions.

1. *dict*

a. _____ a person whose every command must be obeyed; one who rules harshly

b. _____ a message or law announced from a king

c. _____ books that contain words of a language

d. _____ to speak about the future

e. _____ to speak in opposition

2. *fuse*

a. _____ the act of moving blood from one person to another

b. _____ to remove the starter from a bomb

c. _____ to separate and spread out in all directions

d. _____ the state of being mixed-up

e. _____ to reject; to decline

f. _____ rejecting; declining

g. _____ the putting together of different things

F **Dictionary Entries.** Fill in the missing words from your list to complete these alphabetical lists.

I confuse	II diction	III perfection
_____	_____	_____
_____	_____	_____
_____	_____	_____
_____	_____	_____
desire	extended	requires

86

G **More Work with Meanings.** Check your Glossary for definitions.

1. *port*

a. _____ able to be moved from one place to another

b. _____ sent out of a country

c. _____ things brought into a country

d. _____ bringing or repeating information

e. _____ the act of forcing a person to leave a country

Let your Glossary be your guide to word meanings: It will never lead you wrong!

2. *fect*

a. _____ fondness, love

b. _____ being completely or fully right

c. _____ a person who leaves his country to join the enemy

d. _____ being capable, efficient; producing a desired result

e. _____ result; to bring about a change

f. _____ a weakness, a flaw or blemish (Write

_____ two words.)

H **Bible Search.** Check the references below in a New Testament. Write the word from the verse that has a root of fect, fuse, dict, or port.

II Cor. 7:15 _____   Heb. 11:24 _____

II Cor. 6:8 _____   Rom. 12:2 _____

Acts 19:32 _____   I Cor. 16:9 _____

James 5:16 _____   I Cor. 13:10 _____

I **Write About It.** "You shall be perfect, just as your Father in Heaven is perfect" (Matthew 5:48). While we often think *perfect* means to be without error, fault, or sin, the real meaning is to be complete or whole. Paul said we can be perfect in Christ. He is our Savior, and He gives us everything we need to be complete. Read Hebrews 13:20-21. In your own words, tell what these verses mean.

_____

_____

_____

Be sure to record your scores.

safety
lying
onions
sympathy
honesty
you've
gymnasium
systems
billion
recycle
loosely
crystal
purity
bloody
resupply
yearn
Olympic
rhyming
symptom
youthfulness

A **Working with Y.** All of this week's words use the y either as a letter or sound. Group your list words below.

y says y as in *year*

y says long e as in *mighty*

y says short i as in *syllable*

y says long i as in *by*

i says y as in *million*

Go back and trace around each word to make your own Word Forms; then lightly shade the words in each section a different color.

Make Word Forms below for your Home Base Words. Have a friend fill them in correctly. Enter these words in your Word Bank.

B **Seeking Sounds.** Study the words below and notice the sound y makes, as well as the y sound made by i.

multiply	enemy	yoke	flying	cry	cycle
million	canyon	lady	peculiar	tardy	opinion
synagogue	bicycle	city	fancy	hymn	young

1. Use a yellow pencil to circle all the words above in which a y says y, as in *year*.
2. Use a green pencil to put a square around all the words above in which a y says long e, as in *mighty*.
3. Use a blue pencil to put an x on all the words above in which a y says long i, as in *by*.
4. Use a red pencil to put a triangle around all the words above in which a y says short i, as in *syllable*.
5. Use a purple pencil to write y on any i that says y.

C **Sounds of Silence.** Usually the h at the beginning of a word is sounded, but sometimes it is silent. Find four words below which begin with a silent h, and write them on the lines.

healthy	honesty	hire	hedge	handsome	honorable
herb	horror	hero	habit	homage	heifer

_____   _____   _____   _____

D **Synonyms.** Find list words which are synonyms for the following words.

1. glass

2. sign

3. desire

4. reuse

5. arena

6. protection

7. truthfulness

8. untruthful

9. sinlessness

10. compassion

> Learning a variety of words with similar meanings will make your conversations clearer and more interesting.

E **Contractions.** Write contractions for the following:

1. you have _____

2. you would _____

3. you will _____

4. you are _____

safety
lying
onions
sympathy
honesty
you've
gymnasium
systems
billion
recycle
loosely
crystal
purity
bloody
resupply
yearn
Olympic
rhyming
symptom
youthfulness

F **Go for Third.** Look at the two words listed and decide how they are related. Find a list word which is related in the same way.

thousand, million, _____

Nationals, Trials, _____

tissues, organs, _____

infancy, toddler, _____

roomy, unconfined, _____

carrots, radishes, _____

poetry, stanzas, _____

we've, they've, _____

provide, stock, _____

gory, massacred, _____

1,000
1,000,000
1,000,000,000

G **Pyramids.** Use your list words to build the word groups. The first one has been done for you. Be careful; sometimes you have to change a letter to add a suffix.

love
lovely
lovable

pure
im_____

supply
_____ing

honest
dis_____

blood
_____ed

system
_____atic

_____
sympathetic
un_____tic

youth
_____ful
_____

cycle
_____d

90

H **Did You Know?** Acts 5:1-11 tells the story of Ananias and Sapphira, a husband and wife who joined the early believers. They sold their property and gave the money to the church; but they secretly kept part of the money for themselves. Ananias brought their gift to Peter. Write a summary of the story here.

We sold our property and we're giving it all to the Lord!

_____

_____

_____

_____

_____

_____

_____

_____

_____

_____

_____

The sin of Ananias and Sapphira was not in holding back some money, but in lying to God in their hearts. God hates lying! (Proverbs 12:22)

I **Lying or Laying.** *Lying* is a form of *lie*. It can mean telling an untruth, or it can mean stretching out on the bed or ground. A confusing word is *laying,* which means placing something down. The object which is placed is mentioned when *laying* is used. Use these two words in the sentences below.

1. The children were punished for _____ .

2. Aaron is _____ a book on each desk.

3. Newton was _____ under a tree when an apple fell.

4. _____ is a terrible habit.

5. Joe keeps _____ the rake on the ground.

6. The farmer's hens were not _____ enough eggs.

7. The boys were _____ down for a nap.

J **Write About It.** Use a sheet of your own paper to tell about a time when you lied to someone and got caught. Tell how you felt and what the consequences were. What did you do to make it right? Did you learn a good lesson?

She often *lies* about what she *lays*!

kindergarten teacher
manager
athlete
preacher
lifeguard
physician
employment
druggist
scientist
typist
sketch artist
inventor
travel agent
salesclerk
banker
businessman
homemaker
machinist
missionaries
librarian

A **Associations.** Match one of your list words with the picture below which might be associated with that occupation.

Before I formed you in the womb I knew you; Before you were born I sanctified you; I ordained you a prophet to the nations.
(Jeremiah 1:5)

B | **Help Wanted.** All of this week's words relate in some way to job opportunities. Below is a sample page of the classified advertisements. The name of the job title has been left out. Decide what job from your list words will complete the ad and write the word on the line provided.

The Daily Bugle

_____ OPPORTUNITIES

for a little league team. Will travel and make all arrangements.	for a local swim club. Must be expert swimmer.	for a small church. Must be born again.
All-around _____ who can participate in many field events.	for a clinic. May need to work long hours.	for department store. Flexible hours.
for a chain of pharmacies. Will work with prescriptions.	for a company with the latest gadgets. Must have new ideas.	for local corporation. Must have degree in accounting.
for a small office. Must be fast and accurate.	for Christian school. Must like books.	for airlines. Many benefits for someone who is going places.
needed all over the world. Must share Christ.	for local tool company. Must have experience with moving parts.	for laboratory. Will try to find cure for certain diseases.
for advertising company. Bring samples of drawings.	for Christian school. Half days, working with five-year-olds.	for savings and loan company. Must balance accounts.

C | **Rhymes.** Find the list words which rhyme with the following:

1. tanker _____

2. position _____

3. teacher _____

4. visionaries _____

5. meanest _____

6. enjoyment _____

kindergarten teacher
manager
athlete
preacher
lifeguard
physician
employment
druggist
scientist
typist
sketch artist
inventor
travel agent
salesclerk
banker
businessman
homemaker
machinist
missionaries
librarian

D **Alliterations.** When you write a phrase or sentence using the same beginning sound several times, you have *alliteration*. Fill in the following silly sentences with a list word which begins with the same repeated sound. You will have to add an apostrophe and s to show possession.

Example: The <u>cat's</u> claws caught the curtains.

1. The _____ prayers prevented people from prying into problems.

2. The _____ busy bookkeeper bounced back from Boston.

3. The _____ house had happy hearts and helpful hugs.

4. The _____ situation seemed severe to several students.

5. The _____ able aunt acted acutely acrobatic.

6. The _____ daily duties delighted the daffy dogs.

7. The _____ lovely living room had the latest lockers.

8. The _____ model made mailmen mad at members.

Write three more alliterations using other list words or Home Base Words.

_____

_____

_____

E **Guide Words.** Place the list words which would fall between the following guide words in alphabetical order.

machine

_____

_____

_____

please

politics

_____

_____

scream

shake

_____

_____

unite

F **Did You Know?** God called Jeremiah to be a prophet before he was even born. You also are called by God to do something for Him which no one else can do. He is working in your life even now to prepare you for that task. You need to be willing to listen for His call and do what He asks.

G **Write About It.** Do you have any idea what God is calling you to be? Write about what you would like to be when you are an adult. Explain why and describe what you are doing now to help prepare yourself for the task. Remember, whatever you are, God expects you to be a positive witness for Him.

_____

_____

_____

_____

_____

H **Acrostic.** Use the clues to fill in the acrostic.

1. a person who catalogs books in the library
2. a person whose job is to watch the beach
3. a pharmacist
4. a person who thinks up and makes something new
5. a person in charge of something
6. a person trained in games, sports, etc.
7. a person who uses a typewriter
8. a person who sells in a store
9. a job, occupation
10. a person who makes arrangements for tourists
11. a person who prepares children for first grade

1. _____ ☐ _____ _____ _____
2. _____ ☐ _____
3. _____ _____ ☐ _____
4. _____ ☐
5. _____ ☐ _____
6. _____ ☐ _____
7. _____ ☐ _____
8. _____ ☐ _____
9. _____ ☐ _____
10. _____ _____ ☐ _____
11. _____ ☐ _____

The letters in the boxes going down spell _____, a person who works in a company.

dictionaries
decision
position
furniture
perfectly
affect
safety
lying
appreciate
description
confusion
onions
manager
athlete
suggestion
mission
transporting
preacher
lifeguard
substantial
issue
parachute
gymnasium
physician
you've

A **Review Ti and Si.**

1. Write your words which have the following sounds and spellings.

tion says shən as in *salvation*

sion says shən as in *admission*

sion says zhən as in *division*

tion says chən as in *question*

2. Add tion or sion to these roots. Be careful. You may need to change the spellings.

decide

describe

suggest

confuse

3. Write the root words for the follow ing. Be careful. You may need to change the spellings.

confession

notion

rotation

comprehension

When the root word ends in _____, drop the _____ before adding _____ or _____. Sometimes you also have to change a _____ when you add _____ or _____.

4. Change the following as instructed.

        + tion   + al

educate

intend

B Review I and U Following Consonants.

1. Write your words with the following sounds and spellings.

t before i says ch as in *question*

_____

c before i says sh as in *special*

_____

t before u says ch as in *capture*

_____

ch before u says sh as in *chute*

_____

s before u says sh as in *sure*

_____

> **I** suggest that **U** review daily.

In these words the sh sound is spelled _____U , _____U, or _____I.

The ch sound is spelled _____U or _____I.

C Clues. Write a word which is indicated by the following clues.

a place for sports	idea or proposal	objects for a home
not telling the truth	mix-up	done without error
word books	influence	placement
value or cherish	edible root bulbs	carrying

D Word Building. Write list words that fit each train car. Add at least one more word using each root.

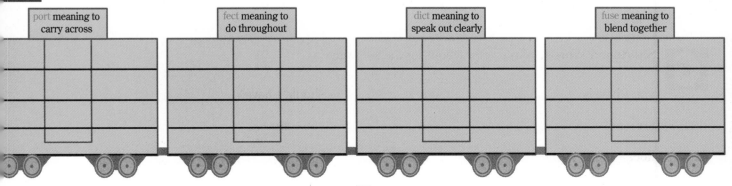

port meaning to carry across	fect meaning to do throughout	dict meaning to speak out clearly	fuse meaning to blend together

dictionaries
decision
position
furniture
perfectly
affect
safety
lying
appreciate
description
confusion
onions
manager
athlete
suggestion
mission
transporting
preacher
lifeguard
substantial
issue
parachute
gymnasium
physician
you've

E **Effect or Affect?** Remember that *effect* means a result. *Affect* means to influence. Select one of the following words and use it correctly in a sentence below:

affect	effect	affection	effective

1. What _____ will the rain have on the crops?

2. It will _____ how fast they grow.

3. My family shows lots of love and

   _____ .

4. Mr. Scott is an _____ leader in our school.

Effect means a result. *Affect* means to influence.

F **Review Spellings and Sounds of Y.**

1. Write the list words with the following sounds and spellings.

   y says y as in *year* _____

   y says long e as in *mighty* _____ _____

   y says short i as in *syllable* _____

   y says long i as in *by* _____

   i says y as in *million* _____

2. Use *lying* and *laying* correctly in the following sentences.

   We saw Mike _____ the package on the shelf.

   My niece is _____ down for a nap.

   Your _____ will get you in trouble.

   The chickens are _____ plenty of eggs.

G **Shortened Words.** Write contractions for the following:

you + have = _____   should + have = _____

are + not = _____   you + are = _____

does + not = _____   it + is = _____

H **Looking to the Future Again.**

1. Match a list word with each of the following descriptions.

one who preaches   one in charge

_____   _____

a doctor   one trained in sports   one who watches at a beach

_____   _____   _____

2. Write words from Lesson 23 which will complete each sentence. Don't forget to use an apostrophe to show possession.

The _____ lab has modern equipment.

The _____ cash register was not working.

The _____ books are organized on the shelves.

Mothers share recipes in their _____ club.

The _____ drawings won first place in the art contest.

I **Picture This.** Write the words which these picture clues indicate.

_____   _____   _____   _____   _____

J **Proofreading.** The wrong form of a word has been used in each sentence. Find it and write the correct form on the line.

We appreciative all your help.   The school held a seminar on bicycle safely.

_____   _____

I received the May issuance in July.   The play-offs will be held in the gymnastics.

_____   _____

The managing called a meeting for nine o'clock.   They are transportation the oil by freighter.

_____   _____

There is substantiate evidence to support creation.   There was confused about the date.

_____   _____

K **Write About It.** In I Thessalonians 1:2-3, we are reminded to appreciate those who help and train us. Think of someone who has had a strong influence in your life. It could be your parents or grandparents, or perhaps a pastor, friend, or teacher. Write that person a letter. State specifically what he or she has done that you appreciate.

climate
medicine
practice
services
imagine
definite
obtain
favorite
adjective
active
purchase
entertain
private
delicate
message
noticeable
uncertain
raged
aggravate
compromise

A **Seeing the Form.** When a word has a vowel-consonant-e pattern, or a vowel-vowel-consonant pattern, the vowel is usually long. However, in an unaccented syllable, the vowel will usually be short or schwa. All of this week's words have one of these two patterns. Write your words in the following forms. The shaded portion in some of the words indicates a long vowel spelling pattern, but a short vowel or schwa pronunciation.

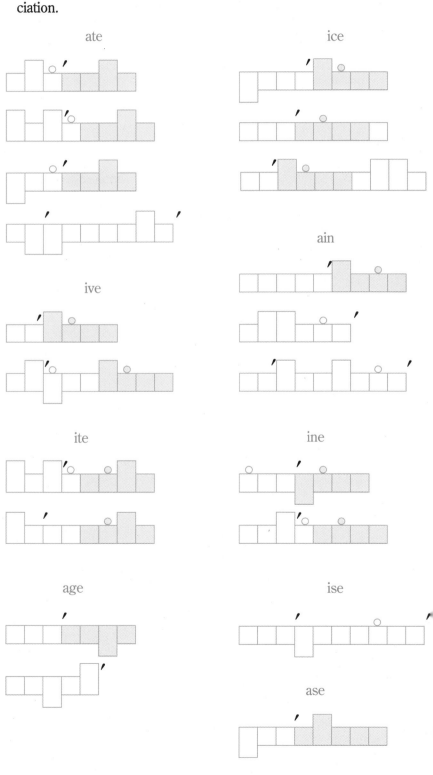

ate

ice

ive

ain

ite

ine

age

ise

ase

B **What's the Origin?** Several of your words come from ancient origins.
Look at the following descriptions and write the correct list word on the line provided.

1. from Italian *favorito,* meaning to favor _____

2. from Latin *privatus,* meaning belonging to oneself _____

3. from Old French *rabia,* meaning madness _____

4. from Greek *klima,* meaning region _____

5. from Latin *compromittere,* meaning to promise together _____

6. from Latin *adjectus,* meaning to add to _____

7. from Latin *servus,* meaning a slave _____

8. from Greek *prassein,* meaning to do _____

9. from Latin *actus,* meaning a doing _____

10. from Latin *imaginari,* meaning image _____

This work isn't as hard as I thought!

C **Choose a Word.** Choose a word from the box to complete each sentence.

Note the difference in the words *promise* and *compromise.* The pronunciation of mise depends on the accented syllable.

active	adjective	definite	climate
delicate	compromise	favorite	practice
private	uncertain	noticeable	

1. The lace has a _____ pattern.

2. The board is having a _____ meeting.

3. The outcome of the trial is _____.

4. I am wearing my _____ dress.

5. She is an _____ member of our church.

6. Our next _____ is Tuesday.

7. Both companies signed the _____.

8. There has been a _____ change in your behavior.

9. My father's decision is _____.

10. A word that describes a noun is an _____.

11. Their _____ allows them to grow crops year round.

Don't Forget! Add your Home Base Words to the Glossary.
101

climate
medicine
practice
services
imagine
definite
obtain
favorite
adjective
active
purchase
entertain
private
delicate
message
noticeable
uncertain
raged
aggravate
compromise

Many Services. The word *service* can be used in many ways. Match the meaning below with the way *service* is used in the following sentences.

a. armed forces branch	f. meeting for worship
b. branch of government	g. money paid for using something
c. business for helping	h. place for getting gasoline, etc.
d. entrance for servants or merchants	i. ready to help
e. helpful	j. street for local or specified traffic

_____ 1. I am <u>at your service</u>.

_____ 2. Can I be <u>of service</u> to you?

_____ 3. Brad will join <u>the service</u> when he graduates.

_____ 4. Please use the <u>service door</u> when you deliver the package.

_____ 5. Shelli's babysitting <u>service</u> is growing.

_____ 6. Carolyn will take a <u>civil service</u> test.

_____ 7. The early <u>service</u> has fewer in attendance.

_____ 8. They use the <u>service road</u> when they check the grounds.

_____ 9. The <u>service station</u> is closed on Sunday.

_____ 10. There is a <u>service charge</u> if you use the credit card.

Morning Services
9:00 and 10:00

Crossword Puzzle.

Across
1. to get
8. describes a noun or pronoun
9. acted uncontrollably angry
10. substance for healing

Down
2. annoy
3. have as a guest
4. fragile
5. not sure
6. a communication
7. to buy

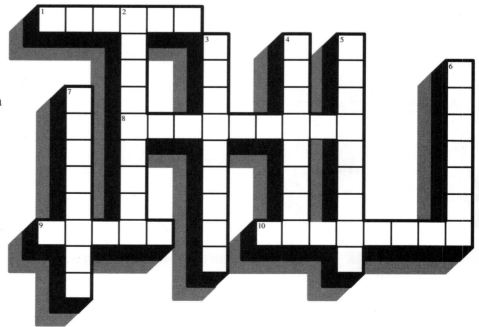

F **More News From Argentina.**

Dear Tom,

I just got your letter. It is good to hear how (activ) you've been at church. It is now summer here. We've discovered how hot the (climit) can be!

We recently went to the capital to (purchus) (medacin) and other supplies, and we were also able to (obtane) a generator for electricity. I got to eat my (favrit) food, hamburgers,

We continue to witness to patients at the clinic, Several of them have attended (servises). We have a (notisable) increase in number. (I magen) our surprise when ten of our patients appeared, It is important that they understand the (messej) of Jesus,

Your friend, Mike

1. Help Mike proofread his letter. He has circled several words which are misspelled. Write them correctly below.

_____

_____

_____

_____

_____

_____

_____

_____

2. Add correct punctuation everywhere you see a caret (∨ , ∧).

G **Dialogue Journal Writing.** Mike mentioned that his family purchased a generator. They needed one because they were often without electricity. Missionaries frequently have to do without things which we would consider necessities. Using a sheet of paper or stationery, do the following:

1. Write about something you would find it difficult to do without. Tell why.
2. Have an adult friend or relative respond to what you wrote and perhaps tell something he or she would not like to do without.
3. Write about something unpleasant you would have to learn to put up with, such as snakes, spiders, or cold showers.
4. Have the same person respond to your writing.
5. Many missionaries have had to sacrifice their lives in order to try to reach people for Christ. How do you feel about that?
6. Have your adult person respond to you again.

business
finish
government
happiness
easily
afterwards
necessary
refusal
faithfully
ministry
disposal
righteous
curiosity
possibility
security
published
heavier
skiing
terrific
workmanship

A **Word Endings.** Suffixes are word endings which add meaning and allow us to use a word in another way. Write a list word after each related word below.

easy		right	
busy		faith	
publish		dispose	
heavy		happy	
secure		work	
refuse		govern	
curious		ski	
after		possible	
minister		final	

B **Unusual Roots.** Four of your words have Latin root words that you may not recognize. Study each root and add the list word.

1. *fini* - to reach the limit or end

2. *necesse* - obligation to duty, need

3. *terror* - to cause trembling, from fright or surprise

4. *bysig* - to be busy, occupied, working

C **Switch-Ups.** Adding suffixes to some words requires spelling changes. Find some examples of these principles:

1. Change y to i.

2. Drop a silent e.

D **Syllable Sense.** Complete these words by writing the syllables. When you finish, trace over them one more time.

[ ] ern	busi [ ]	
[ ] sar [ ]	[ ] fus [ ]	
[ ] ful [ ]	heav [ ] [ ]	[ ] ing
[ ] cu [ ]	[ ] si [ ] [ ]	fin [ ]
[ ] os [ ]	dis [ ] [ ]	[ ] pi [ ]
[ ] ic	[ ] try	right [ ]
pub [ ]	[ ] man [ ]	
[ ] ter [ ]	eas [ ] [ ]	

Choose three Home Base Words and write them in the same way, leaving syllables for a friend to fill in. Make your entries into the Word Bank.

E **Replacements.** Use a list word to replace these numbered definitions in the story below.

Moses' 1. _____ to follow sin was honored

by God. He 2. _____ led the children of

Israel, giving them laws which established a

3. _____ and a place of worship. This

allowed them to be 4. _____ before God. He

taught them that if they wanted 5. _____, it was

6. _____ to obey God.

His 7. _____ lasted more than forty years.

8. _____, he died on Mount Nebo. The

first five books 9. _____ in the Bible con-

tain Moses' writings. Thank God for this wonderful servant of the

Lord.

1. denial	6. required
2. loyally	7. act of serving
3. system of laws	8. later
4. without sin	9. printed
5. joy	

business
finish
government
happiness
easily
afterwards
necessary
refusal
faithfully
ministry
disposal
righteous
curiosity
possibility
security
published
heavier
skiing
terrific
workmanship

F **Class Action.** The two words given are related in some way. Decide how they are related and complete these classes of words with one of your list words.

1. wrote, printed, _____

2. running, skating, _____

3. office, store, _____

4. Congress, legislature, _____

5. garbage, trash, _____

6. service, work, _____

7. joy, gladness, _____

8. loyally, regularly, _____

9. later, then, _____

10. denial, declination, _____

G **Analyze Your Words.**

1. Find list words which are synonyms for the following:

wonderful _____   effortlessly _____

protection _____   inquisitiveness _____

skill _____   complete _____

2. Find list words which are antonyms for the following:

sinful _____   nonessential _____

start _____   lighter _____

improbability _____   sadness _____

H **Picture This.** Look at these three pictures; then write the word on the line provided.

 sk ng

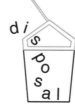

I **Did You Know?** A *minister* was originally a servant. Joshua was a minister to Moses. In Jeremiah, God calls the priests His ministers. This term carried over to the New Testament Church where the minister is a servant of God. This is an honor, for Christ Himself is said to have come not to be ministered to, but to minister. Write a description of a good minister you know.

_____

_____

_____

_____

_____

_____

_____

J **Word Find.** Fourteen of your list words are hidden in the puzzle. Circle them; then write them on the lines provided.

```
A B I S E C U R I T Y
N F S S E N I S U B T
E I T R E F U S A L I
C N O E S K I I N G L
E I T E R R I F I C I
S S E N U W O R K A B
S H Y L I S A E L S I
A Y T I S O I R U C S
R L A S O P S I D Y S
Y H A P P I N E S S O
W O R K M A N S H I P
```

_____   _____

_____   _____

_____   _____

_____   _____

_____   _____

_____   _____

_____   _____

K **Made By Him.** Ephesians 2:10 says, "We are His workmanship, created in Christ Jesus unto good works." It is God's delight as the Master Builder to take His children and make them clean and useful for His glory. God never gives up on us. Remember you can sing, "He's still working on me." Maybe someone you know is discouraged. Make a card, or use stationery, and write a cheerful note to that person. You can include Ephesians 2:10 or Philippians 2:13 in your note.

Under Construction
Loving Father
Bldg. Co.
Permit No. Eph. 2:10

Be sure your scores have been recorded.

difference
importance
absence
tremendous
advantage
horrible
entrance
delicious
sensible
convenient
courteous
intelligence
industrious
numerous
obedient
generous
courageous
nutritious
deliverance
reasonable

A **Suffixes.** All of your list words have common suffixes that expand their meaning or change their use in a sentence. For example, the suffix may change the word from a verb to a noun. Print your words according to their suffixes. Note the shaded boxes in each section.

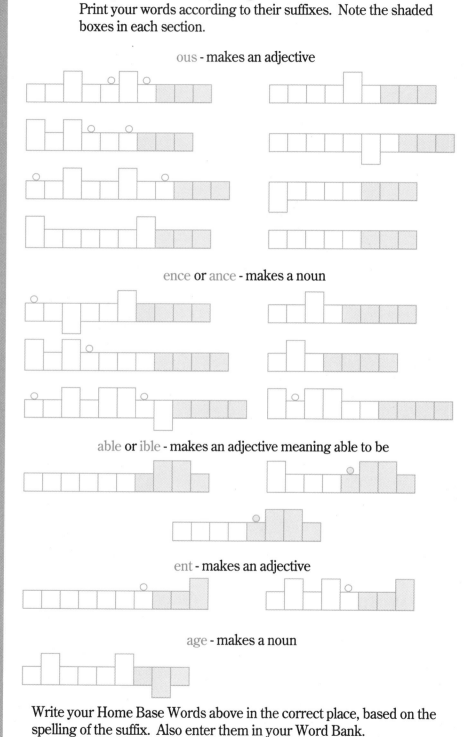

ous - makes an adjective

ence or ance - makes a noun

able or ible - makes an adjective meaning able to be

ent - makes an adjective

age - makes a noun

Write your Home Base Words above in the correct place, based on the spelling of the suffix. Also enter them in your Word Bank.

This page will help you in studying this week's words. Go back and study each shaded area and each syllable. Using a different color for each set of suffixes, write over each printed word in cursive.

Word Relatives. Many of your words have the same root word as other common words. Fill in a list word on the first line and a related word that you know on the second line. You may use a dictionary if needed.

FAN TAS TIC!
LESSON
27

_____ _____ deliverer

_____ _____ entry

_____ _____ courageously

_____ _____ unimportant

_____ _____ nonsensical

_____ _____ differently

_____ _____ obedience

_____ _____ absently

_____ _____ nutrient

Increase your word family. Get to know your relatives.

Wendy Word

C

Adding Your Adjectives. Complete each sentence with an adjective from your list.

1. When the quarterback uses good sense, he is a _____ player.

2. When a film is filled with great horror, it has many _____ scenes.

3. When I obey my teacher, I am an _____ student.

4. When a hospital has a great number of doctors, it has _____ physicians.

5. When your food has enough nutrients, you are eating _____ meals.

6. When Bobby showed courage in pulling the girl out of the water, the newspaper reported his

    _____ deed.

7. After our principal heard all our reasons, he agreed that we had a _____ plan.

8. Mrs. Birky commented on Marie's courtesy to the visitors. She said, "You were a very

    _____ young lady."

9. In an industry, employees must work hard. The boss is pleased to have

    _____ workers.

10. We tasted many delicate cookies and candies at the party. We enjoyed all the

    _____ food.

difference
importance
absence
tremendous
advantage
horrible
entrance
delicious
sensible
convenient
courteous
intelligence
industrious
numerous
obedient
generous
courageous
nutritious
deliverance
reasonable

 Alphabetizing. Alphabetize five list words between the guide words in each block.

1. abdomen

_____

_____

_____

_____

courtesy

2. decide

_____

_____

_____

_____

horizon

3. horn

_____

_____

_____

_____

nurse

4. nurture

_____

_____

_____

_____

triumph

 Knowing Your Nouns. Complete the meanings with a list word.

1. To put yourself in a better position over another person is

   to take _____ of him.

2. The place to enter is the _____ .

3. To be delivered and set free is a _____ .

4. To be of great value is to be of _____ .

5. Lack of attendance or presence is _____ .

6. Great mental ability is _____ .

7. Being unlike the others is a _____ .

It is of great *importance* to find the
entrance to *deliverance*. It will really
make a *difference*!

F **Synonyms and Antonyms.** Find a list word which is a synonym for each of the following:

benefit _____ diligent _____

wonderful _____ terrible _____

brave _____ healthy _____

unselfish _____ tasty _____

Find a list word which is an antonym for each of the following:

bothersome _____ few _____

unreasonable _____ stupidity _____

similarity _____ exit _____

presence _____ insignificance _____

G **Write About It.** This lesson has several words which are positive character qualities. Some are listed in the box.

industrious	reasonable	courteous
courageous	generous	intelligent
obedient	sensible	

Choose one and write about it. Tell what you think the character quality means from a Christian viewpoint and give at least three reasons why you think it is an important quality.

_____

_____

_____

_____

Write another paragraph telling about a time when you or someone you know displayed this character quality.

_____

_____

_____

_____

Use the margins to write the name of a person you know who demonstrates each quality listed.

conforming
deformed
formal
format
inform
informative
misinformation
performance
performed
transformation
transformed
abruptly
corruption
disrupting
eruption
incorruptible
interruption
rupture
construct
construction
destroyed
destruction
indestructible
instruct
instructor
obstruct
obstruction
reconstruction
restructured
structured

A **Base Words.** All of your list words are built from Latin words with these three parts: form, rupt, and struct. Check the list and write the root next to the meaning. Check the Glossary if you need help.

_____ to break

_____ to build, order, or arrange

_____ to shape or mold

B **Constructing Structures.** Complete each sentence to use a spelling word in context. Use a word built from the root in parentheses. Use your Glossary as needed.

1. We enjoyed the _____'s science lecture. (*struct*)

2. The President attended a _____ dinner party. (*form*)

3. The driver _____ swerved to miss the child. (*rupt*)

4. All the carpenters had to wear hard hats at the _____ site. (*struct*)

5. Television is often full of _____ and wrong ideas. (*form*)

6. The water company repaired the _____ in the pipe. (*rupt*)

7. All the hats and flags will _____ the view of the people behind us. (*struct*)

8. Amy worked carefully to draw out the _____ for her project. (*form*)

9. All of the noise was _____ our classes. (*rupt*)

10. We all enjoyed the _____ of the musicians who visited our school. (*form*)

Verb Sense. Word building usually begins with knowing the meaning of the verb form of a word. The verbs below are related to your list. Match them to their meanings. Write the verb on the first line, and then write a related word to each verb on the second line.

interrupt	transform	instruct	conform	construct	inform
obstruct	erupt	perform	destroy	disrupt	corrupt

Example: ___structure___ to put in order ___restructured___

_____ 1. to play a part in a drama

_____

_____ 2. to keep something from taking place as arranged

_____

_____ 3. to break down cells; to decay

_____

_____ 4. to build up by putting everything in order

_____

_____ 5. to change completely _____

_____ 6. to break up and out, sometimes with force _____

_____ 7. to break into a conversation _____

_____ 8. to tell about; to shape thoughts _____

_____ 9. to teach; to arrange ideas

_____

_____ 10. to take on the shape; to mold

_____

_____ 11. to break up; to bother; to throw into confusion

_____

_____ 12. to tear down, to ruin, to do away with

_____

113

conforming
deformed
formal
format
inform
informative
misinformation
performance
performed
transformation
transformed
abruptly
corruption
disrupting
eruption
incorruptible
interruption
rupture
construct
construction
destroyed
destruction
indestructible
instruct
instructor
obstruct
obstruction
reconstruction
restructured
structure

D **Life Eternal.** Paul states, "So also is the resurrection of the dead. The body is sown in corruption, it is raised in incorruption" (I Corinthians 15:42). Paul describes our corruptible bodies. These are our earthly bodies that get hurt, become ill, grow old, and die. However, your new Heavenly body is incorruptible. It cannot die but will live forever. Write I Corinthians 15:51-52 in your best handwriting.

E **Build On It.**

1. Remember struct means build. Use a form of struct in the following sentences. Use the Glossary, if needed.

   a. The company was _____ when the new president took office.

   b. This is one _____ that remained after the tornado hit here.

2. Remember form means shape. Use a form of form in the following sentences. Use the Glossary, if needed.

   a. The potter threw away the _____ clay pot and started over again.

   b. The pamphlet was written to _____ the parents of the new policies.

   c. The senior boys will need to wear tuxedos to the _____ banquet.

   d. Our lives are _____ when we receive Christ.

F **Dialogue Journals.** Write about the first topic below. Ask someone to respond to what you wrote. Then write back and forth on the other two topics.

   1. What the Corruptible Body on Earth is Like

   2. Why I'm Glad Jesus Will Give Us New Bodies

   3. What the Incorruptible Body Looks Like and Can Do

114

G **Building Forms.** Now that you know the more familiar meanings of your verbs, you can write list words by their parts. The first one is done for you. Remember the roots: form = shape; struct = build, order, arrange; rupt = break. Hint: Write in the root first, then check your list.

1. into/between + break + a process

interruption

4. separate + break + being

2. put into + shape + quality of

5. not + down + order + able to

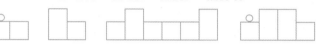

3. change + shape + process

6. through + shape + act of

H **Write About It.** Choose a phrase from each pair listed below and use it in a sentence.

1. destroyed by a hurricane/ a volcanic eruption

2. disrupting noises/ informative film

3. a great instructor/ a super performance

4. a sudden interruption/ abruptly spoke

5. terrible destruction/ amazing construction

Your scores need to be entered on the graph.

settlement
innocent
accident
proof
objection
prejudice
process
jury
legal
complaint
honorable
trial
conviction
courtroom
judges
evidence
plaintiff
defendant
attorney
guilty

A **Courtroom.** Below is a possible floor plan for a typical courtroom. Place the following labels where they belong.

courtroom	plaintiff	defendant	jury
attorney	judge	public seating	

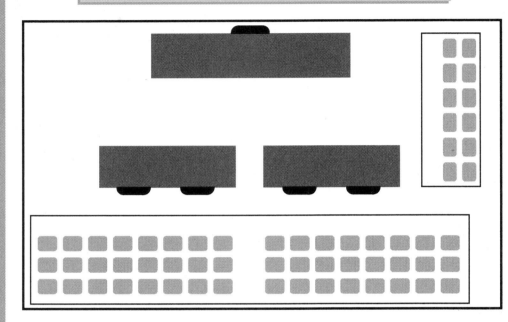

B **Scrambled Syllables.** Unscramble the following syllables to form list words. Leave out one syllable.

tri u prej dice

ment cess tle set

ac dent ci ble

vict tor ney at

tion con ence vic

com fend de ant

i ob dence ev

ble hon ment a or

cent no in tion

ob tion jec vict

> *Now you are light in the Lord. Walk as children of light.*
> (Ephesians 5:8)

 Mixed-Up Letter. Bob wrote a letter to Jim about a recent field trip. The only problem is he used wrong words or a wrong form of a word eight times. Help him correct the letter by writing the correct words above the incorrect ones. He also needs to add quotation marks around a direct quote.

Dear Jim,

    Our class recently visited a trial room, where a trying was in its final day. The defender was brought in. Everyone stood as the judging entered the room. The attornal for the defense went through the processing of making his closing remarks to the juris, who then left to establish a verdict. When they returned, the spokesman said, We find the defendant not guiltful. It was an exciting trip for all of us.

                         Your friend,

                         Bob

 Triplets. Use the three clues to discover which list word should be added to complete the group.

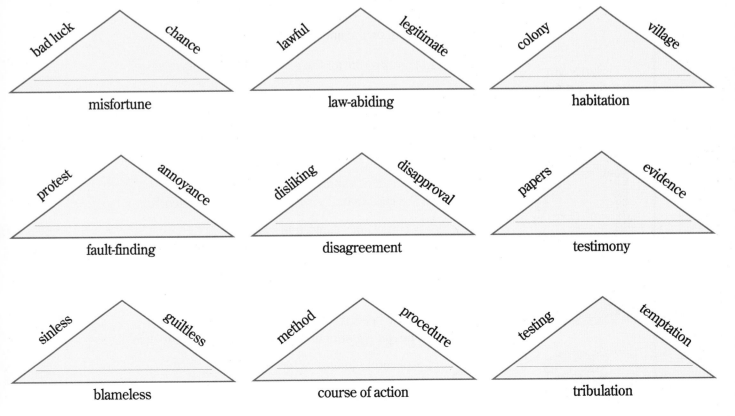

bad luck / chance	lawful / legitimate	colony / village
misfortune	law-abiding	habitation

protest / annoyance	disliking / disapproval	papers / evidence
fault-finding	disagreement	testimony

sinless / guiltless	method / procedure	testing / temptation
blameless	course of action	tribulation

117

settlement
innocent
accident
proof
objection
prejudice
process
jury
legal
complaint
honorable
trial
conviction
courtroom
judges
evidence
plaintiff
defendant
attorney
guilty

 Rhyming Couplets. The following pairs of phrases need a list word which rhymes with the word at the end of the first phrase.

1. It was the lawyer's prediction

   he would receive a _____.

2. The suspect made a goof

   when he left behind some _____.

3. Our family's _____

   went on a long journey.

4. Wherever he trudges,

   he finds many _____.

5. The king, while looking quite regal,

   wanted everything thoroughly _____.

6. Without any constraint,

   she stated her _____.

Write a couplet for one of your Home Base Words.

Synonym study is a super source for sentence assembly!

 Improving Vocabulary. Each of the sentences below has an italicized word. You may or may not know its meaning, but it is a synonym for one of your list words. Choose the list word which means the same. Write the word on the line provided.

1. The *advocate* for the plaintiff prepared his case well.

   attorney   defendant   jury   _____

2. There was enough *documentation* to convict the suspect.

   judges   prejudice   evidence   _____

3. The *bigotry* in the community caused strife among the citizens.

   accident   attorney   prejudice   _____

4. The jury wanted a *condemnation* of the defendant.

   complaint   conviction   jury   _____

5. His *virtuous* behavior was obvious to the other students.

   guilty   innocent   honorable   _____

6. Christ will judge everyone who appears at His *Judgment Seat.*

   jury   courtroom   settlement   _____

7. The *complainant* brought charges against the defendant.

   plaintiff   judges   attorney   _____

Did you add your Home Base Words to your Glossary?

118

G **Write About It.** You are a Christian who has been brought to trial. The charge against you is simply that you are a believer. Actually, you want to be found guilty of being a Christian. Is there enough evidence to convict you? Write all the proof that anyone might find that will prove you are a follower of Christ.

_____

_____

_____

_____

H **Rebus.** Look at the puzzle and write a sentence based on I Timothy 4:12 which is illustrated.

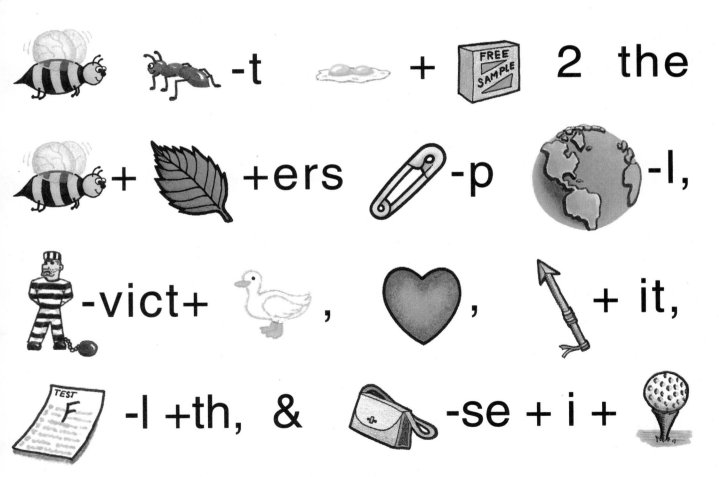

business
climate
finish
medicine
importance
absence
settlement
accident
services
government
tremendous
horrible
proof
definite
performance
adjective
happiness
objection
construction
prejudice
easily
convenient
abruptly
misinformation
destroyed

A   **Accented and Unaccented Long Vowel Spellings.**

1. Place your words beside the correct vowel-consonant-e pattern.

ate _____   ice _____

ive _____

ine _____   ite _____

> These words have a vowel-consonant-e pattern which usually indicates a _____ vowel. However, they are in unaccented syllables, causing the vowel to be _____ or schwa.

2. Write words with the following origins. Choose from *active, adjective, climate, favorite, imagine,* and *raged.*

Original Word	Meaning	
Latin, *adjectus*	to add to	_____
Latin, *actus*	a doing	_____
Italian, *favorito*	to favor	_____
Old French, *rabia*	madness	_____
Greek, *klima*	region	_____
Latin, *imaginari*	image	_____

B   **Review Suffixes.**

1. Add ed and ing to the following root words.

service _____

entertain _____

aggravate _____

compromise _____

obtain _____

> When you add ed or ing to a word that ends in silent e, drop the e.

2. Write your words with the following roots:

easy _____   busy _____

happy _____   govern _____

One word has the Latin root fini, meaning to reach the limit.

Write it. _____   Write another related word. _____

3. Find words from your list or from a previous lesson in this unit with these suffixes:

ed _____   al _____   ity _____

ment _____   ly _____   ness _____

er _____   eous _____   ible _____

ing _____   ent _____   ance _____

tion _____   es _____   ence _____

4. Adding a suffix often changes the part of speech. Write the following list word changes:

An ous makes an adjective.

_____

An ence or ance makes a noun.

_____

_____

An ible makes an adjective.

_____

An ent makes an adjective.

_____

5. Find the following from a previous lesson in this unit:

Adding able makes it able to have a reason.

_____

Adding age makes a noun of *advance*.

_____

An eous or ious changes a noun to an adjective.

_____

_____

_____

6. Complete these sentences:

When I obey, I am

_____.

When I use good sense, I am

_____.

Food with nutritional value is

_____.

I can change both the spelling and part of speech!

Fix-bot

business
climate
finish
medicine
importance
absence
settlement
accident
services
government
tremendous
horrible
proof
definite
performance
adjective
happiness
objection
construction
prejudice
easily
convenient
abruptly
misinformation
destroyed

A great review gets to the root of the matter.

Word Building.

1. Write a list word and another related word with the following roots:

   rupt meaning to break _____ _____

   struct meaning to build _____ _____

   form meaning to shape _____ _____

2. Check Lesson 28 and complete each sentence with a form of the word in parentheses.

   The propaganda was full of _____. (form)

   The _____ of the volcano surprised everyone. (rupt)

   Teachers _____ their students. (struct)

   The tornado _____ several buildings. (struct)

   A caterpillar undergoes a marvelous _____ when it becomes a butterfly. (form)

   The program ended _____. (rupt)

Under Construction. To *construct* is to make or build. Usually builders take their tools and materials and make something which is strong. God is also a builder. He takes lives which are yielded to Him and makes them better and stronger. He is never finished, however. He works with us for our entire lives, shaping us into a "building" which is pleasing to Him. Think of an area in your life where the Lord is working to make you stronger. Write about it on the lines below. Read Philippians 1:6. Is this true in your life?

_____

_____

_____

_____

_____

_____

_____

_____

_____

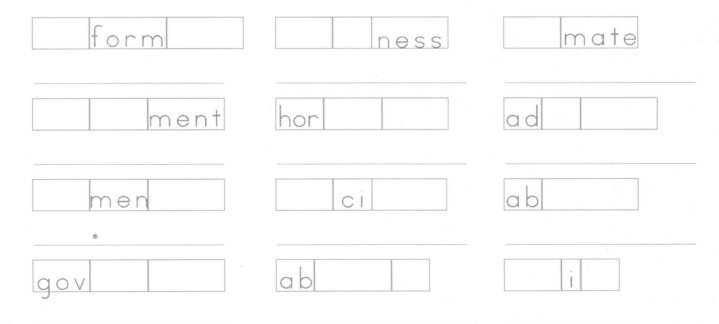

Revisiting Court.

1. Write list words to complete the following paragraph.

   Recently, a case was held in court involving an _____

   claim. When the jury was selected, one attorney made an _____

   because he detected _____ in one of the jurors. That juror was dismissed.

   As _____ of the defendant's innocence accumulated, the plaintiff decided to drop some of

   the charges, and a _____ was made out of court.

2. Write a word from Lesson 29 which will complete the series.

   sinless, guiltless, _____

   annoyance, protest, _____

   lawful, legitimate, _____

   method, procedure, _____

   moral, virtuous, _____

Word Forms and Respellings. Fill in the boxes below. Part of each word has been filled in for you.
Rewrite the word on the line.

form	ness	mate
ment	hor	a d
men	ci	ab
gov	ab	i

It's time to enter your scores for this lesson and the six weeks on your graph.

minute
record
guessed
except
cellar
sense
bass
vain
ceiling
wring
prophet
dessert
hoarse
wound
forth
foul
heal
diary
suite
mantel

A **Work with Words.**
Some of this week's words are members of a homophone pair. Write your word that is a homophone for each of the following:

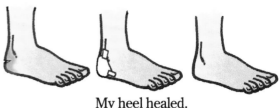

My heel healed.

1. sealing _____

2. cents _____

3. horse _____

4. mantle _____

5. sweet _____

6. guest _____

Desert is a homograph. It has two pronunciations (de sert′ and des′ert). It is often confused with *dessert*. Look these words up in your Glossary. Decide which to use in the following sentences. Write *de sert′*, *des′ert*, or *dessert* on the line provided.

1. The _____ receives little rain.

2. I always enjoy cake for _____.

3. If you _____ me, I will probably get lost.

4. We tried to choose a _____ from the menu.

5. The hikers were lost in the _____ for four days.

It helps to remember that the ss in dessert can stand for *super sweet*!

    d   e   s   s   e   r   t
            u   w
            p   e
            e   e
            r   t

Diary and *dairy* are often confused.

Which one is associated with daily milking? _____

Which one would I write in? _____

124

B **Separating Pairs.** Choose the correct word in parentheses for each sentence below. Write the correct word on the line provided. Use your Glossary as needed.

1. The Old Testament a._____ was not always respected. Often the people did not b._____ from his warnings because they refused to listen to him. (profit, prophet)

   a. _____ b. _____

2. The captain chose his a._____ battalion to go b._____ into the battle. (forth, fourth)

   a. _____ b. _____

3. Mrs. Smith a._____ that the b._____ list would have one hundred names. (guessed, guest)

   a. _____ b. _____

4. Joan could not a._____ the fact that everyone was invited b._____ her. (accept, except)

   a. _____ b. _____

C **I Accept All Except One.** Fill in the sentences with the correct word from the Word Bank.

1. He _____ the gift.

2. Use any color _____ blue.

3. We saw everything _____ the Grand Canyon.

4. We are _____ in the beloved (Eph. 1:6).

5. We must _____ Christ to be saved.

6. There is no _____ to the rule.

Remember these meanings:
cept = take
ac = to
ex = out
Therefore:
accept = to take
except = take out

Word Bank		
accept	accepted	exception
accepting	except	exceptional

D **Chameleons.** The following pairs of words are homographs. They have two pronunciations. The glossary respelling is given. Write the word correctly beside its respelling; then write a short definition for each word.

1. bas _____

   bās _____

2. wo͞ond _____

   wound _____

3. rek′ ərd _____

   ri kȯrd′ _____

4. min′ it _____

The singing bass sang bass.   mī nūt′ _____

minute
record
guessed
except
cellar
sense
bass
vain
ceiling
wring
prophet
dessert
hoarse
wound
forth
foul
heal
diary
suite
mantel

Pair Some Pears. Each of the following sentences contains a homophone of a word that can be used to complete the sentence. Write the pair of homophones.

1. The bride's mother was so sweet. She had sent flowers to the bridal _____.

   _____   _____

2. I heard the phone ring before I could _____ all of the water out of the sponge.

   _____   _____

3. The Thanksgiving fowl became _____ after sitting out for several hours.

   _____   _____

4. I hurt my heel while running, but if it will _____ quickly, I can run again on Monday.

   _____   _____

5. Uncle Frank yelled at the horse so loudly he became _____.

   _____   _____

6. Mark was sealing the _____ of the clubhouse with a new kind of paint.

   _____   _____

Meanings Check.

1. Look up *vain, vane,* and *vein* in your Glossary. Use one of them correctly in each sentence below.

   a. The _____ showed the wind blowing from the northeast.

   b. A varicose _____ results in poor blood circulation.

   c. Miss Ling tried in _____ to locate her lost keys.

   d. The old miner searched for a _____ of silver.

2. Look up these pairs of homophones in a dictionary: *cellar/seller, sole/soul,* and *mantel/mantle.* Write the correct homophone under each picture.

G **Did You Know?** God chose Solomon to build His temple. It took seven years to complete, and it was finished and dedicated in the eleventh year of Solomon's reign. During the dedication ceremony, Solomon prayed to God. After his prayer, fire came down from Heaven and consumed the burnt offering, and God's glory filled the temple. After the ceremony, God appeared to Solomon at night and gave him a very special promise for His people. This promise is found in II Chronicles 7:14. Read it.

What four things must God's people do in order to be heard by Him?

_____

_____

_____

What will be God's response?

_____

_____

_____

H **Write About It.** Israel was not always obedient to God; so God had to judge His people. Think about our own nation. There are some ways we disappoint God. We are not as righteous as He would like us to be. Write about some of these areas, and give the solution for our nation based on II Chronicles 7:14. Use some of your spelling words or homonyms of your words as you write.

_____

_____

_____

_____

_____

_____

_____

Home Base Words and scores should be entered in their appropriate areas.

column
whether
banquet
scissors
debt
echo
phrase
pneumonia
castles
muscle
equipment
wholesale
knives
straighten
receipt
liquid
sponge
backache
balm
scratching

A **Get the Picture.** Because many of your words have silent letters, remembering how the word looks will help you spell it correctly. Complete the Word Forms below. A silent letter should be placed in the shaded box. After you print the letters, rewrite the word on the line.

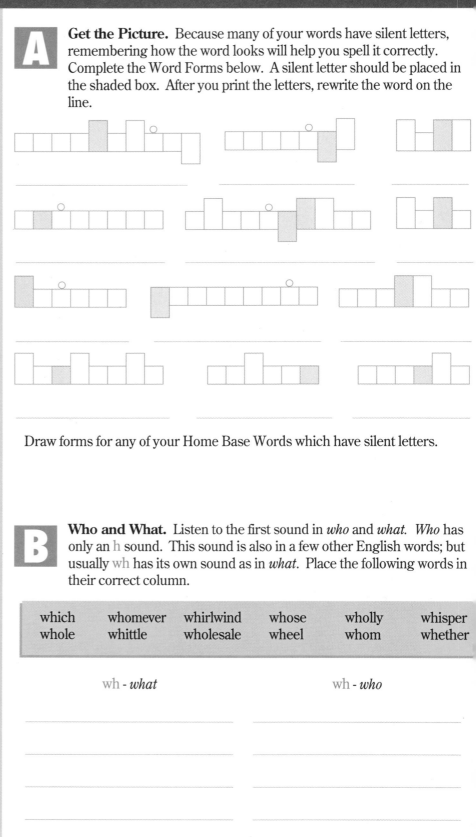

Draw forms for any of your Home Base Words which have silent letters.

B **Who and What.** Listen to the first sound in *who* and *what*. *Who* has only an h sound. This sound is also in a few other English words; but usually wh has its own sound as in *what*. Place the following words in their correct column.

| which | whomever | whirlwind | whose | wholly | whisper |
| whole | whittle | wholesale | wheel | whom | whether |

wh - *what*   wh - *who*

C Reviewing Digraphs and Clusters.

1. The digraph qu has its own sound pronounced kwh. Fill in your three qu words.

_____   _____   _____
         tools   fluid   large dinner

2. The digraph ch usually has the sound pronounced in *church*. However, some English words use ch to say k as in *school, Christ,* and *chorus*. Write two more ch words from your list.

_____   _____

3. The digraph ph is another spelling for f. Write your list word and two more words that begin with ph.

_____   _____   _____

4. The final ge says j, known as soft g. The nge cluster has its own blend. Write your list word which has nge; then complete the other words which have nge.

_____   stra_____   hi_____   lu_____   da_____r

5. *Balm* is an older English word which has almost disappeared from our language. However, understanding its spelling helps with several other words. Place these words with their meanings below.

a part of your hand

_____

a healing oil

_____

an offering or gift to the poor

_____

"The Lord is my shepherd."

_____

a quiet, easy feeling

_____

a type of tropical tree

_____

> calm
> palm
> alm
> Psalm
> balm

6. Find two list words which are compounds. Write and divide the two words by drawing a line between the syllables.

_____

_____

129

column
whether
banquet
scissors
debt
echo
phrase
pneumonia
castles
muscle
equipment
wholesale
knives
straighten
receipt
liquid
sponge
backache
balm
scratching

D

Related or Different? Fill in a list word which is an antonym for these words.

snack _____   huts _____

bend _____   solid _____

silence _____   retail _____

Fill in a list word which is related to these words.

sentence _____   rubbing _____

influenza _____   sound _____

medicine _____   pain _____

money owed _____   bone _____

make neat _____   if _____

forks _____

E

Picture This. Fill in the word that names the picture.

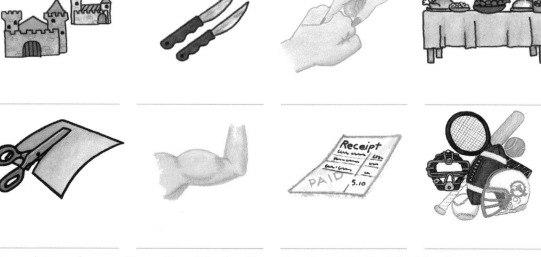

Draw pictures for your Home Base Words. Also enter them into the Word Bank.

F   **Did You Know?** The Greek word *pneuma* meant air, wind, breath and blow. It is the root for *pneumonia,* an infection of the lungs which causes breathing problems. However, *pneuma* has a very important meaning in the New Testament. It refers to the Spirit of God. II Peter 1:21 tells us that men of God wrote Scripture as they were breathed upon by the Holy Spirit. Thus, we can fully trust every word of the Bible to be just exactly what God wanted, without error, and totally true.

G   **Putting It Into Words.** Write a note to God thanking Him for His wonderful Book, the Bible. Include at least three reasons why you are thankful for His Word.

Dear Lord,

H   **Working Smart.** Fill in a list word to complete these sentences.

1. Kings live in _____.

2. A seamstress uses _____.

3. Butchers use _____.

4. Highway repairmen use heavy _____.

5. A chef prepares a _____.

6. A salesclerk writes a _____.

7. The weight lifter strained a _____.

8. A deep-sea diver could collect a _____.

9. A collection agent tries to collect a _____.

10. A doctor finds the cause of a _____.

11. A chemist works with an unknown _____.

12. A pharmacist fills prescriptions for bronchial _____.

increase
arrive
exchange
prevent
excitement
distance
excuses
previous
invention
extra
delivery
accuse
enforce
occurred
supersonic
submitting
impolite
dissatisfied
preferred
nonsensical

A **Before the Fact.** Complete each item with a word from your list.

1. Super means above, and sub means below.

   _____ is above the speed of sound.
   _____ is to come under authority.
   Check your Glossary or a dictionary for one more word for super and sub

   _____   _____

2. Im, dis, and non all mean not or without. Fill in these opposites.

   satisfied _____

   sensible _____

   polite _____

> Prefixes are word parts added to the beginning of a word. They always add to or change the meaning of a word.

3. In means within or to cause within. It can be spelled en. Write three list words with this prefix.

   _____

   _____

   _____

4. The prefix ex usually means outward or above. Write four list words with this prefix.

   _____   _____

   _____   _____

5. The prefix pre usually means before. Write three list words with this prefix.

   this prefix.   _____

   _____   _____

6. The prefix ad means to; but it can be spelled many ways, with the d changing to the first letter of the next syllable. Complete these words.

   ar_____   ac_____

            oc_____

7. The prefix de refers to listing or putting down as in *details*. Write your

   de word. _____

8. Another meaning for dis or di is to separate, as in *divide* or *distract*.

   Write your dis word. _____

B **Meanings Match.** Write in your words that match these meanings. Use your Glossary, if needed.

_____ happening before

_____ liked most

_____ stop

_____ mail service

_____ not pleased

_____ blame

_____ obeying

_____ happened

_____ rude

_____ silly

_____ to add more

_____ switch

_____ reach

_____ reasons

_____ something new

_____ make sure it's obeyed

Be careful; you may have to make spelling changes when you join syllables!

C **Assembly Required.** Put the word parts together and place the correct word in the blank to complete the sentence.

ex cite change tra ment	1. Mrs. Jones wants us to have an _____ pencil. 2. Will you _____ papers with me? 3. The _____ of seeing the clowns thrilled the kindergarteners.
pre in vent ion ed	1. Quick thinking _____ the accident. 2. People laughed at Mr. Edison's _____ . 3. Don't let teasing _____ you from doing the right thing.
ac ex cuse es ed	1. Mark had many _____ for being late. 2. Ryan _____ Andy of taking his pencil. 3. "Do not falsely _____ your brother."
dis satisfy tance ed action	1. Jamie ran the farthest _____ . 2. Mrs. Jobe's _____ with us was evident. 3. Mom is _____ with the dress she bought Saturday.

increase
arrive
exchange
prevent
excitement
distance
excuses
previous
invention
extra
delivery
accuse
enforce
occurred
supersonic
submitting
impolite
dissatisfied
preferred
nonsensical

It's Not There. In means *not* when it is added before certain root words. Match the following *in* words with their definitions below.

inaudible	ineffective	indecent	inadequate
incurable	inactive	inadvisable	incorrect
	incapable	indefinite	

not enough _____

not able _____

not proper _____

not recommended _____

not moving _____

not right _____

not able to be heard _____

not correctable _____

not sure _____

not producing results _____

Syllable Stacks. Write in the syllables for the stacks below; then rewrite the word on the line. Remember to study each syllable as you write it.

liant
bril
ly
i
nar
di
or
tra
ex

sen

son	

liv	

curred

tance

ferred

mit

po

cite

vi

tra

force

rive

crease

F

Did You Know? *Super* is a word that has been in man's language since before the days of Christ. It occurs in Latin, French, Spanish and English, and means above or over. Many, many words in our language use this word as a prefix. Look at the descriptions below and write in a *super* word. Check a dictionary if you need help.

1. more than *natural* _____

2. to *visually* oversee something _____

3. a person who *tends* to another's work _____

4. faster than sound, creating a *sonic* boom _____

5. to *impose* one photograph over another _____

G

Write About It. The Book of Hebrews teaches that Christ is *superior* (from *super*) to all others. Check these references from Hebrews and name some things that Christ is better than.

1:4 _____   3:3 _____

7:27 _____   8:6-7 _____

Read Colossians 1:18 and tell why Christ should be superior in your life.

_____

_____

_____

_____

H

Nonsensical Nonsense. Choose or make adjectives and nouns from your list and add them to the words below. The funnier and more nonsensical they are, the better! Choose one of your phrases and draw its picture in the frame.

_____ Kittens

_____ Dragon

_____ Submarine

An Elephant's _____

An Unbelievable _____

The Unusual _____

Write a short paragraph about your title and picture on notebook paper. Remember that your scores are to be recorded each week.

135

complaining
explanation
plainly
unexplained
compress
depressed
expressive
impression
pressure
pressurized
suppress
accountable
accountant
counters
discount
recount
attend
attendant
attentive
extend
intended
intention
tendency
assignment
design
designate
resignation
resigned
signals
signatures

A

Base Words. Your word list is built on five basic root words. They are plain, press, count, tend and sign. Check your list and match the root to its meaning. Write the root word on the line. Check the Glossary if you need help.

_____ to push down steadily

_____ to motion or write a message

_____ to lean toward or stretch toward something

_____ to be clear and easily understood

_____ to tell one by one

B

Related Words. Write a list word that is from the same family as the one listed below.

explain	intentionally
expression	pressured
designated	counting
complained	accounting
assigned	attention
extension	attended
impressive	resign

Just For Fun. What is the relationship between the word *assignment* and the following sentence? *"The noble elephant marched near Goshen, Indiana,"* *said Sam's aunt.*

Write sentences showing the same relationship for two of these words: *signatures, accountant, complaining* or *explanation.*

1. _____

2. _____

C Word Study.

1. The prefix ad means to, or to do. Its spelling can change with the d becoming the first letter of the next syllable. For example, ad + cept = *accept;* ad + point = *appoint.* Write your six ad words.

_____   _____   _____

_____   _____   _____

2. The suffix sion or tion means the process of doing an action. Write ion words next to the related ing word.

resigning _____   explaining _____

intending _____   impressing _____

3. Two of your words refer to people who do something. Write the two words.

_____   _____

4. Note some of your words change their spelling although their meaning stays the same. This often happens in our language and the changes must be memorized. Write examples of these changes below, based on the clues given.

tend ⟶ tent   plain ⟶ plan

attend _____   explain _____

intend _____

5. The one-syllable word *sign* has a silent g. You can remember this g by knowing related words in which the g is not silent. Divide your *sign* words into the following two lists.

silent g   sounded g

_____   _____

_____   _____

_____   _____

                                _____

D Prefix Meanings. Match the following prefixes to their meanings by writing the letter on the line. Check your Glossary or dictionary if you need help.

_____ de   a. again   _____ sub   e. with, together

_____ ex   b. not   _____ com   f. inside, within

_____ re   c. out, outward   _____ im/in   g. from

_____ un   d. down   _____ dis   h. under

complaining
explanation
plainly
unexplained
compress
depressed
expressive
impression
pressure
pressurized
suppress
accountable
accountant
counters
discount
recount
attend
attendant
attentive
extend
intended
intention
tendency
assignment
design
designate
resignation
resigned
signals
signatures

E **Match Up.** Write list words to complete the following meanings:

1. _____ signing again, this time to quit

2. _____ pressing inward

3. _____ to take a percent away when something is on sale

4. _____ the setting forth of a clear reason

5. _____ to draw or set down an idea

6. _____ to reach out your arm rather than pull it in

7. _____ to pull under or hold down something

8. _____ not described

9. _____ to push down with a clean cloth, your hand, or other instrument

10. _____ had in mind to do; planned

11. _____ pulled down with bad feelings

12. _____ outwardly showing feelings

F **Picture This.** Write 15 of your words in their matching forms below. Some of the letters are filled in for you. Trace over the provided letters as you write, and then trace around each form once.

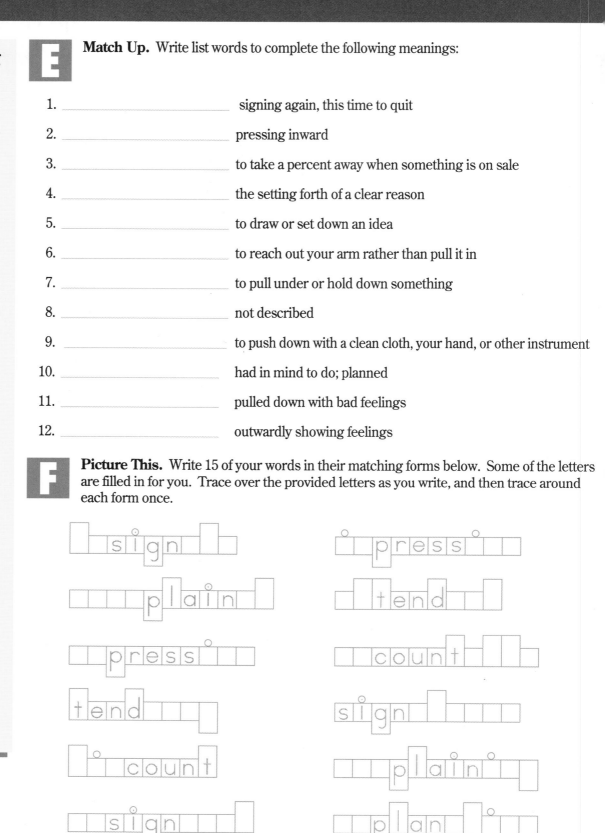

138

 Did You Know? *Accountable* means able to give a reason for or a telling of what we have done. Write Romans 14:12 here. Draw a pretty border around the verse.

_____

_____

Who must give an account? _____

To whom must the account be given? _____

In salvation, Christ gives us His righteousness and does not count our sins against us. However, after we are saved, God holds us accountable for the way we live. Read the verses below. Name some things we are accountable for and will be judged for.

Luke 16:2 _____

Matthew 5:22 _____

Romans 2:16 _____

I Corinthians 3:13-15 _____

 Dialogue Journal. Write a paragraph to complete this statement: "Knowing I am accountable to God, I want to live…." Make the paragraph as long as you like; then ask a parent, teacher, or friend to respond. Write back and forth two or three times in a written conversation about this topic. If you need additional room, use paper or stationery.

_____

_____

_____

_____

_____

_____

_____

_____

_____

_____

_____

_____

guard

protection

soldier

lieutenant

forces

liberty

troops

defense

authority

colonel

sergeant

commander

 in chief

hijacking

hostage

strict

corps

officers

escaped

regiment

loyalty

A **Picture This.** Find your list words which will fit the following configurations. Some of the boxes have been shaded because they contain unusual spellings. Look at them carefully.

B **Hostages.** Fill in the following story with list words or forms of list words. Clues have been given.

An interesting hostage story occurred in 1976, in Entebbe, Uganda, Africa. Entebbe is a major city in Uganda, and its airport is a main stop between Europe and South Africa. In 1976, (soldiers)_____ from Palestine (seized)_____ a French airplane and forced it to land at Entebbe. They held 100 (captives)_____ who were on the plane, most of them citizens of Israel. Israeli (authorities) _____ began making plans for a daring raid; and a week later, Israeli (military power)_____ attacked the airport. The Palestinian (protection)_____ was no match for the Israelis. All the hostages (became free) _____ except three who were killed in the crossfire. The Israeli (army men) _____ had risked their lives for the (freedom) _____ of 100 citizens.

C **Analogies.** Complete each of the following analogies with one of your list words.

1. Superintendent is to school system as _____ is to armed services.

2. Truthfulness is to honesty as faithfulness is to _____ .

3. Slave is to bondage as _____ is to captivity.

4. Prisoner take-over is to prison as _____ is to plane.

5. Watchman is to factory as _____ is to prison.

6. Team is to league as _____ is to army.

7. Protect is to attack as _____ is to offense.

D **Rank.** Put the following in their order of authority from greatest to least. Use the Glossary, if needed.

| soldier | lieutenant | colonel | sergeant | commander in chief |

1. _____   4. _____

2. _____   5. _____

3. _____

guard
protection
soldier
lieutenant
forces
liberty
troops
defense
authority
colonel
sergeant
commander in chief
hijacking
hostage
strict
corps
officers
escaped
regiment
loyalty

 Hink Pinks. Look at the descriptions below. Find a list word that fits part of the clue; then add a word that rhymes with the list word to complete the answer. Write the two-word phrase on the line.
For example: An *unhappy boy* is a *sad lad*.

1. daily writings of an officer whose rank is like a naval captain

2. an organization of people who do the same work, involved in armed battle

3. a tough person who protects

4. a joining of those who shield from danger

5. liquid foods for groups of soldiers

6. chosen as strongly enforcing rules

7. cavalry animals for military power

 Acrostic. Complete the following acrostic with the clues given.

1. serviceman

2. strongly enforcing rules

3. got away

4. to defend

5. a shelter

6. freedom

7. armament

8. faithfulness, devotion

9. a police officer below captain

10. power to command

11. an officer in the military above a sergeant

142

G **Liberty.** Most people place a high value on their freedom. Describe liberty by making an acrostic of the word. Each letter of *liberty* should begin a word that reminds you of its meaning. If you cannot think of a word which begins with a letter, use a word which contains the letter.

L _____

I _____

B _____

E _____

R _____

T _____

Y _____

H **Write About It.** Jesus said the peacemakers are blessed and that they would be called sons of God. Paul said God has called us to peace, we should pursue the things which make peace, and we are to live peaceably with all men. How can we do that? Write about how you as an individual can live at peace with others or how a nation can live at peace with other nations. Your Word Bank can provide spelling assistance. Be sure your Home Base Words have been entered in your Glossary.

_____

_____

_____

_____

I **Allegory.** An allegory is a story in which characters and objects are symbols for other people and things. Paul used an allegory in Ephesians 6:11-17 to explain how a Christian can be strong in the world. Complete the following paragraph with list words based on that Scripture.

Christians are involved in a battle called life. The Christians who are fighting the battle are like

_____. God is our supreme leader, or _____.

We wear armor as our _____ against Satan's attacks. We even have a shield,

which is a _____ from his arrows. Each church is like a military division, or

_____; and the leaders in the church are some of our military leaders, or

_____. Our final expert, or _____, for all decisions is our

sword, the Bible, which is the Word of God.

minute
increase
column
except
whether
cellar
exchange
scissors
prevent
guard
sense
debt
muscle
pressure
attend
design
soldier
sergeant
wring
liberty
occurred
submitting
explanation
colonel
accountant

A **Homonym Review.**

1. Write a list word and its homophone to label each picture.

Go
it!

_____   _____   _____

2. Use *accept* or *except* correctly in each sentence.

Please _____ my invitation.

Everyone went to the park _____ my sister.

Did you _____ Christ as your Savior?

3. Write the correct respelling on each line in the sentences.

a. It will take longer than a _____ to find such a

_____ contact lens. (min′ it, mī nūt′)

b. The man with the _____ voice caught the biggest

_____ in the fishing contest. (bas, bās)

c. The school nurse _____ the gauze around the

bleeding _____. (wo͞ond, wound)

d. The sound in the studio must be exactly right when an artist

wants to _____ a

_____.

(rek′ ərd, ri kȯrd′)

B **Silent Letter Review.**

1. The following words have silent letters. Circle the silent letters and rewrite the words.

column _____	scissors _____
debt _____	muscle _____
wring _____	design _____
guard _____	foreign _____
castles _____	pneumonia _____
receipt _____	straighten _____

2. Use *weather* and *whether* correctly in the following sentences.

I don't know _____ I'll be allowed to go.

The _____ has been unusually nice this spring.

3. Circle the words in which wh says its own sound as in *what*. Put an x on the words in which wh says h as in *who*.

which	whomever	whirlwind	why	white
whose	whiskers	whoever	what	whale
wharf	whipping	whatever	wheat	whole

 C **Prefix Review.** Write your list words with the following prefixes. Then write another word with the same prefix.

sub meaning below _____

in meaning within _____

ex meaning outward _____

Remember the spelling changes with ad!

pre meaning before _____

ad meaning to _____

145

minute
increase
column
except
whether
cellar
exchange
scissors
prevent
guard
sense
debt
muscle
pressure
attend
design
soldier
sergeant
wring
liberty
occurred
submitting
explanation
colonel
accountant

assignment
unexplained
complaining
extend
plainly
discount
depressed
designate
tendency
recount
intended
compress
signatures
impressive
counters

D **Did You Know?** *Debt* means the obligation to pay, or that which we owe. Romans 3:8-10 says there is one thing we are to owe, and that is love. The Law of God is fulfilled as we love Him and love our neighbors. Write about a way you can love others.

_____

_____

_____

_____

E **Review of Root Words.**

1. Find words with the following base words.

   press - to push down steadily _____

   tend - to lean toward something _____

   sign - to motion or write _____

   plain - to be clear and understandable _____

   count - to tell one by one _____

2. Each design has a word in it. Move the related words from the shaded box to the correct place on the art below.

plain

suppress

attentive

resigned

accountable

146

Military Review. In the first column write list words that match the meanings. In the second column write a word for each unusual spelling.

like a captain in the navy _____

to protect _____

freedom _____

a police officer below captain _____

a man serving in the army _____

gu says g, as in *got* _____

olo says ər, as in *serve* _____

er says är, as in *arm* _____

ieu says o͞o, as in *moose* _____

orps says ȯr, as in *store* _____

di says j, as in *injury* _____

G **Syllable Check.**

1. Assemble the word parts and write the correct word in the sentences. Remember the word parts may change in their spelling.

as de sign ed es	a. The teacher _____ several pages to read.
	b. The _____ in the floor did not match.
	c. The artist _____ the company logo.

de in crease es ing	a. The price of cola is _____ 20 cents.
	b. When the volume _____, we can't hear.
	c. Her pay _____ when she works longer.

ac ex cept ed tion	a. I _____ the invitation immediately.
	b. There seems to be an _____ to the rule.
	c. Everyone had the measles _____ me.

Fifth grade has been a *super* year!

These students have some *great* spelling skills!

Yes, absolutely *awesome*!

Without a doubt! They have done a *terrific* job…

…and developed *fantastic* word power!

They are on an *excellent* path to success in sixth grade!

Be sure to record your scores for the lesson, the six weeks and the year.

Pronunciation Key for English

Consonants

Sound:	Spelling Examples:
b	baby, bubble, bib
ch	child, much, patch, nature, question, ancient
d	day, ladder, sad, played
f	fish, often, off, phone, cough
g	go, wiggle, big, ghost, league
h	hot, hurry, who
j	jump, age, judge, gym, graduate
k	keep, tickle, sick, cup, picnic, choir, antique
l	look, little, tall
m	my, mommy, come
n	no, winner, nine, know
ng	ring, singing
nk	thank, ankle
p	pie, apple, hope
qu	queen, quiet, (combination of kwh)
r	red, rose
s	see, lesson, miss, city, dance
sh	she, wish, sugar, machine, nation, mission, special
t	tie, tattle, eat, walked
th	think, both, (breath)
<u>th</u>	these, either (voice)
v	vase, save
w	we, well (voice)
wh	what, whether (breath)
y	yes, yellow, onion, million
z	zoo, fuzzy, maze, has
zh	measure, azure, vision

Vowels

Sound:	Spelling Examples:
ā	able, date, aid, day, eight, great
a	apple, hat
ä	father (Same sound as short o)
är	arm, far, sparkle, sorry
ē	me, these, keep, meat, chief, lady, valley, ceiling
e	edge, mess, ready, friend
er	errand, berry, bear, care, arrow, January, fair, heir
ī	I, fine, night, pie, by
i	it, his, gym
ir	miracle, here, ear, deer, superior
īr	fire, retire
ō	open, bone, coat, show, soul
o	top, otter, bother
ô	often, soft, also, haul, caught, draw, bought
oi	oil, joy
oo	book, should
o͞o	cool, tube, stew, fruit, group, to
oor	poor, tour
ȯr	for, more, soar, four, forth, door
ou	out, towel
our	hour, power
ū	use, fuel, pew, Europe, beauty, you
u	fun, couple, another, love (This marking is used in an accented syllable; in an unaccented syllable a schwa is used for the same sound.)
ə	alike, independent, nation, marble
ūr	pure, jury, your
ər	summer, third, turtle, dollar, color, earth, journal (This marking is used in accented or unaccented syllables)

5th Grade Glossary

Aa

abruptly ab rupt ly (ə brupt′ lē) adv. suddenly *Josh entered the room abruptly.*

absence ab sence (ab′ səns) n. not here, state of being away, not in attendance *His surgery caused a six-week absence.*

accept ac cept (ak sept′) v. to receive willingly, approve, agree to *We become Christians when we accept Christ as Savior.*

accident ac ci dent (ak′ sə dənt) n. an event which was not planned or intended *We were involved in an accident.* adj. chance *We met by accident.*

account ac count (ə kount′) n. 1. a record of expenses or savings *We have an account at the bank.* 2. an explanation *Dottie gave an account of the accident.*

accountable ac count a ble (ə koun′ tə bəl) adj. responsible for one's actions *We are accountable for every word and action.*

accountant ac coun tant (ə kount′ ənt) n. a person who keeps track of financial records *The accountant was responsible for the financial report.*

accuse ac cuse (ə kūz′) v. blame *Tim tried to accuse his little brother of causing the accident.*

accustom ac cus tom (ə kus′ təm) v. to make a habit, to make used to *Missionaries often have to accustom themselves to new foods.*

achievement a chieve ment (ə chēv′ mənt) n. accomplishment, do something successfully *Shawn's achievement in spelling pleased him and his parents.*

active ac tive (ak′ tiv) adj. 1. showing movement, lively *My little niece is an active child.* 2. being used *My charge account is not active now.*

adjective ad jec tive (aj′ ik tiv) n. a word or phrase which describes a noun or pronoun *Write an adjective here.*

admire ad mire (əd mīr′) v. think highly of, regard with approval, appreciate *We admire honesty in a person.*

advantage ad van tage (əd van′ tij) n. benefit, better position *Our team had the advantage over the opponents.*

advice ad vice (əd vīs′) n. opinion about what to do, recommendation *Mom and Dad want advice about buying a new home.*

advisable ad vis a ble (əd vī′ zə bəl) adj. recommended as good advice *It is advisable to come in out of the rain.*

advisory ad vi so ry (əd vī′ zər ē) adj. having power to recommend *The advisory board meets on Monday.*

affect af fect (ə fekt′) v. to influence *Effort will affect the quality of your work.*

affection af fec tion (ə fek′ shən) n. fondness, love *Their family shows a lot of affection.*

afford af ford (ə fôrd′) v. 1. to have enough money for *You can afford a new couch.* 2. to be able to do something without serious consequences *You can't afford a low grade average if you are going to college.*

afterwards af ter wards (af′ tər wərdz) adv. later than something else *We will have refreshments afterwards.*

aggravate ag gra vate (ag′ rə vāt) v. 1. to make worse *A loud noise can aggravate a headache.* 2. to disturb or annoy *Mike is always trying to aggravate his sister.*

alley al ley (al′ ē) n. a narrow street or passageway *The alley behind our house leads to our garage.*

alternate al ter nate (ôl′ tər nit) adj. every other, one then the other *The Spanish club meets on alternate Mondays.* n. substitute *The coach sent in an alternate.* (ôl tər nāt′) v. to take turns or change places on a regular basis *We will alternate the schedule.*

anchor an chor (ang′ kər) n. 1. a heavy object used to keep a boat from drifting, anything which holds something in a secure position *The anchor was lowered.* 2. the last man on a relay team or tug-of-war team *Jim was chosen as anchor.* v. to hold in place *The men tried to anchor the structure with steel braces.*

angels an gels (ān′ jəlz) n. 1. heavenly beings created by God *A multitude of angels surround God's throne.* 2. people who behave in a pleasing manner *Most children are angels when sleeping.*

angles an gles (ang′ gəlz) n. 1. places where two lines intersect *The walls meet to form angles.* 2. viewpoints *Try to see things from other angles.*

annoy an noy (ə noi′) v. to disturb by repeated unpleasant acts *Don't annoy me by tapping your pencil.*

anonymous a non y mous (ə non′ ə məs) adj. not known, without a name *Our school received a large gift from an anonymous donor.*

answering an swer ing (an′ sər ing) v. 1. replying, responding *The doctor is answering all of my questions.* 2. solving a problem *She is answering all the addition problems.* 3. being responsible *She is answering for her poor decisions.*

anyway an y way (en′ ē wā) adv. anyhow, in any manner *Mrs. Jobes said to draw the picture anyway we wanted.*

apparent ap par ent (ə per′ ənt) adj. 1. easily seen, visible *The city skyscrapers are apparent from my house.* 2. easily understood *The quiz answers were apparent.* 3. seeming to be true *There was an apparent mistake on the bill.*

appear ap pear (ə pir′) v. 1. to come into view *The star will appear in the east.* 2. to come into existence *Flowers appear in early spring.* 3. to seem *They appear to be honest.*

appreciate ap pre ci ate (ə prē′ shē āt) v. 1. to be thankful for *I appreciate your kindness.* 2. to enjoy *I appreciate good music.*

arctic arc tic (ärk′ tik) adj. 1. having to do with the North Pole and the area around it *Polar bears live in the arctic area.* 2. very cold *Cold, arctic air moved into our area.*

area ar e a (er′ ē ə) n. 1. a piece of ground *They built the house in a wooded area.* 2. the measure of a region *Find the area of the space.* 3. part of any surface or a particular zone *Our area has had several tornadoes.*

argue ar gue (är′ gū) v. 1. quarrel, disagree *Don't argue with your brother.* 2. debate *The lawyer will argue his case before the jury.*

arrive ar rive (ə rīv´) v. 1. to come to one's destination *We will arrive there tomorrow.* 2. succeed *By the world's standards, we arrive when we become famous or rich.*

assemble as sem ble (ə sem´ bəl) v. to gather *We will assemble in the auditorium at 1:00.*

assembly as sem bly (ə sem´ blē) n. a gathering for worship, law-making, entertainment *A special assembly was called so we could hear the missionary.*

assignment as sign ment (ə sīn´ mənt) n. a task given to be completed *Jim finished his assignment quickly.*

associate as so ci ate (ə sō´ shē āt, ə sō´ sē āt) v. 1. to have a connection with, as a friend *It is wise to associate with godly people.* 2. to make a connection in the mind *I associate kindness with love.* (ə sō´ shē it) n. a fellow worker *The new business associate made friends easily.*

athlete ath lete (ath´ lēt) n. a person trained in games, sports, etc., which require skill *He is an all-star athlete.*

atmosphere at mos phere (at´ məs fir) n. 1. the mass of air surrounding the earth *The Earth's atmosphere is becoming polluted.* 2. the air in a certain place *The atmosphere gets thinner as you climb a mountain.* 3. the environment *The restaurant's atmosphere was quiet.*

attend at tend (ə tend´) v. 1. to be present at a place or event *We want to attend the graduation.* 2. to care for *The nurse will attend my mom after her surgery.*

attendant at ten dant (ə ten´ dənt) n. one who waits on or cares for *The attendant helped my dad with the gas.*

attentive at ten tive (ə ten´ tiv) adj. 1. pay close attention to *The students were attentive during the demonstration.* 2. thoughtful, courteous *Mother was attentive to her sick daughter.*

attic at tic (at´ ik) n. the room below the roof, and above the ceiling, usually with a sloping ceiling *Our attic is full of our old toys.*

attorney at tor ney (ə tər´ nē) n. lawyer *The corporation has its own attorney.*

authority au thor i ty (ə thȯr´ ə tē) n. 1. power to command, influence *Jesus had authority over nature.* 2. expert *He is an authority on stamps.*

automotive au to mo tive (ȯt´ ə mō´ tiv) adj. having to do with automobiles *I stopped by the automotive department.*

avenue av e nue (av´ ə noo) n. a street *We walked down the avenue to the grocery.*

average av er age (av´ rij, av´ ər ij) n. 1. normal, usual *The results were above the average.* 2. number found by dividing the sum of several digits by the number of digits *The average score was 83.* adj. normal, usual *She is an average student.*

Bb

backache back ache (bak´ āk) n. a pain in the back *His backache kept him awake all night.*

balm (bäm) n. 1. a substance from certain plants which can be used as medicine, an ointment *Balm was recommended for his aching muscles.* 2. anything that soothes *The soft music was a balm for her frazzled nerves.*

banker bank er (bang´ kər) n. a person who owns or manages a company which keeps and loans money *Mr. Johnson asked the banker for a loan to buy his new car.*

banquet ban quet (bang´ quit) n. a meal with lots of food for many people *The banquet was held in appreciation of our teachers.*

bass (bas) n. a fish of fresh or salt water *My brother caught a large bass.* (bās) n. 1. lowest male voice *My dad sings bass in the choir.* 2. a man with a low voice *He is a bass.* 3. a musical instrument with a low range *Sally plays bass violin.*

beauty beau ty (bū´ tē) n. something that looks good, pleasing or attractive *The beauty of Creation is marred by pollution.*

beige (bāzh) adj. tan in color *Dad bought a new beige suit.*

beneath be neath (bi nēth´) prep. below *The box was buried beneath the tree.*

beneficial ben e fi cial (ben ə fish´ əl) adj. helpful *Aspirin is beneficial for reducing fever.*

betrayal be tray al (bi trā´ əl) n. given over to an enemy by disloyalty or deceit *The betrayal of Jesus by Judas saddened the disciples.*

billion bil lion (bil´ yən) n. one thousand million, 1,000,000,000 *Their corporation is worth a billion dollars.*

binders bind ers (bīn´ dərz) n. 1. persons or equipment which hold things together, such as books *The binders at the press went on strike.* 2. detachable covers for holding together sheets of paper *The binders need more paper.*

biographies bi og ra phies (bī og´ rə fēz) n. histories of lives of people *Livingstone's biography was interesting.*

bloody blood y (blud´ ē) adj. containing the red fluid which circulates in the body, covered with blood, bleeding *The Civil War had many bloody battles.*

bruised (broozd) v. injured in a way which caused discoloration, made black and blue *Jesus was bruised for our sin.* adj. injured *He put ice on his bruised knee.*

bugle bu gle (bū´ gəl) n. a brass horn used mainly for military signals *They will blow the bugle at dawn.*

bundle bun dle (bun´ dəl) n. a bunch, several items tied or wrapped together, a package *We carried a bundle of sticks to the fire.*

buried bur ied (ber´ id) v. 1. placed a dead body into the ground *Many soldiers are buried at Arlington Cemetery.* 2. hid in the ground *The treasure was buried in a secluded spot.* 3. covered up, so it was out of view *She buried her face in her hands.*

burst (bərst) v. 1. to explode, to come apart suddenly *When the balloon burst, the baby cried.* 2. to be filled *Lou is about to burst with pride.* n. a sudden action *We had a sudden cloud burst.*

business busi ness (biz´ nis) n. 1. a store, factory *His business has grown rapidly.* 2. sales to customers *Business is booming around Christmas.* adj. having to do with selling *Our house is close to the business district.*

businessman busi ness man (biz´ nis man´) n. a man who owns or runs a company *We are looking for a businessman to sponsor our club.*

Cc

cabinet cab i net (kab´ ə nit) n. 1. cupboard *The cabinet couldn't hold anything else.* 2. a group of advisers to a president *A president chooses his cabinet carefully.*

calculate cal cu late (kal´ kū lāt) v. 1. compute *Did you calculate my bill correctly?* 2. guess *I calculate they will arrive around 2:00.*

calendars cal en dars (kal´ ən dərz) n. 1. systems for arranging the year into days, weeks, and months *We have calendars to remind us of tasks.* 2. schedules *The museum publishes calendars of monthly events.*

calming calm ing (käm´ ing) adj. soothing *The soft music has a calming affect.* v. making quiet *The principal is calming the students.*

canoe ca noe (kə nōō´) n. a narrow boat *We went downstream in a canoe.* v. to move in a narrow boat *We will canoe downstream for two miles.*

carefully care ful ly (ker´ fə lē) adv. 1. safely *Drive carefully.* 2. accurately *Teresa carefully hammered the nails into the frame.*

castles cas tles (kas´ əlz) n. large buildings with thick walls and open spaces, associated with the Middle Ages *We visited several castles in Scotland.*

catalog cat a log (kat´ ə lôg) n. a listing of names, titles, or articles. *The card catalog in the library helps locate books.*

catastrophe ca tas tro phe (kə tas´ trə fē) n. a sudden disaster *The Mexico earthquake was a catastrophe.*

ceiling ceil ing (sēl´ ing) n. 1. the top part of a room, opposite the floor *A chandelier hung from the ceiling.* 2. an official upper limit, as on prices *The government placed a ceiling on oil prices.* 3. the height of the lower part of a cloud covering *The cloud ceiling was 5,000 feet.*

cellar cel lar (sel´ ər) n. a room below ground used for storage *They ran to the cellar when they saw the tornado.*

central cen tral (sen´ trəl) adj. 1. near the center *Let's put the supplies in a central location.* 2. main, most important *The central fire station has three engines.*

cents (sens) n. pennies, several coins, each valued at 100th part of a dollar *The candy was only ten cents.*

century cen tu ry (sen´ chər ē) n. a period of 100 years *He was born in the eighteenth century.*

chalkboard chalk board (chôk´ bȯrd) n. dark colored surface for writing or drawing *The writing on the chalkboard needed to be erased.*

chapter chap ter (chap´ tər) n. 1. a section of a book *You must read one chapter of the book.* 2. an episode, as a chapter of one's life *College will begin a new chapter in Ruth's life.* 3. a branch of a club *Nicole's Girl Scout chapter is very active.* 4. a division of Scripture *We are studying the seventeenth chapter of John.*

checkout check out (chek´ out) n., adj. 1. the place for settling purchases *The checkout lane was crowded due to the sale.* 2. the place in a library for settling which books can be taken *We went through the checkout to get three books.* v. check out *I wanted to check out three books.*

cherish cher ish (cher´ ish) v. 1. to love *The couple vowed to cherish one another.* 2. to treasure *We cherish our freedom.*

chest (chest) n. 1. a box with a lid, usually for holding something special *She keeps her diary in a chest.* 2. a cabinet with drawers for keeping clothes *The chest matches the dresser.* 3. the part of the body enclosed by ribs *William has a chest cold.*

chillier chill i er (chil´ ē ər) adj. colder *It was chillier this morning than yesterday.*

chilly chill y (chil´ ē) adj. cool *The weather is chilly.*

choices choi ces (choi´ səz) n. 1. acts of choosing *We made several choices from the menu.* 2. a large enough number for selection *He has many choices to make.*

chores (chȯrz) n. jobs *He does his chores before school.*

citizens cit i zens (sit´ ə zənz) n. 1. people who belong to a country, usually by birth, give loyalty to it, and have certain privileges *U. S. citizens have many freedoms.* 2. people who live in a particular city, town, or state *A meeting of the citizens was called by the mayor.*

climate cli mate (klī´ mət) n. the average weather of a region *Areas on the equator have a warm, humid climate.*

cocoa co coa (kō´ kō) n. 1. powdered chocolate *She added cocoa to the recipe.* 2. a drink made by adding water or milk to powdered chocolate *The fudge recipe calls for cocoa.*

coconut co co nut (kō´ kə nut) n. the fruit of a tropical palm tree *We added coconut to the frosting.*

coffee cof fee (kôf´ ē) n. a drink made by brewing the ground beans of a special plant *We enjoy a cup of coffee with dessert.*

collar col lar (kol´ ər) n. 1. the part of a shirt which goes around the neck *This collar is too small for my neck.* 2. a piece of leather for an animal's neck *The dog's collar is blue.* v. to seize or capture *The store manager tried to collar the thief before he left the store.*

collection col lec tion (kə lek´ shən) n. 1. things gathered together *Building a stamp collection can be an interesting hobby.* 2. money gathered during a church service *The ushers counted the collection.*

colonel colo nel (kər´ nəl) n. an officer ranking below a brigadier general, like a captain in the navy *He was recently promoted to colonel.*

column col umn (kol´ əm) n. 1. a tall narrow structure for supporting a building *When the column fell, the building collapsed.* 2. anything with a tall, narrow shape *Put your answer in the correct column.* 3. a section in a newspaper *She writes a column for the daily newspaper.*

combine com bine (kəm bīn´) v. to mix together *You need to combine the ingredients thoroughly.* (kom´ bīn) n. a machine for harvesting grain *A combine is an expensive machine.*

comfort com fort (kum´ fərt) v. to console in time of grief *I tried to comfort my friend.* n. 1. encouragement *Her presence was a comfort.* 2. anything that makes life easier *Electricity is a comfort some people don't have.*

command com mand (kə mand´) v. to give orders to, to have authority over *The captain will command the troops.*

commander in chief com man der in chief (kə man´ dər in chēf) n. the highest authority of the armed services *The President is our commander in chief.*

comment com ment (kom´ ent) n. a remark or statement about something *Mrs. Smith made an interesting comment in my journal.* v. to make a remark *The Senator will comment on the new budget plan.*

commercial com mer cial (kə mər´ shəl) n. a paid advertisement *The commercial interrupted the program.* adj. having to do with trade *Jason's dad works for a commercial airline.*

common com mon (kom´ ən) adj. usual, ordinary *Rough roads are common in rural areas.* n. belonging to or used by everyone *The first Christians had all things in common.*

compassion com pas sion (kəm pash´ ən) n. sympathy or sorrow due to suffering of another *Jesus looked at the crowd with great compassion.*

complaining com plain ing (kəm plān´ ing) v. telling of pain, faults, problems *Complaining is a bad habit.*

complaint com plaint (kəm plānt´) n. the act of finding fault, being annoyed, or telling of pain *Mom wrote a complaint to the store.*

complete com plete (kəm plēt´) adj. finished, whole *The pieces make a complete picture when put together.* v. to finish *I was unable to complete the assignment.*

compound com pound (kom´ pound) n. a substance made by combining two or more parts or elements *Salt is a compound.* (kəm pound´) v. to increase or make more serious *Your anger will compound the situation.*

comprehension com pre hen sion (kom´ prē hen´ chən) n. knowledge gained by understanding *It seems your comprehension of the subject is incomplete.*

compress com press (kəm pres´) v. to press together, to push down with a clean cloth *Compress the wound to stop the bleeding.* (kom´ pres) n. a cloth used to apply pressure *This hot compress will ease the soreness.*

compromise com pro mise (kom´ prə mīz) n. an agreement in which each side gives up something *Both parties agreed to the compromise.* v. 1. to make an agreement by giving up something *We'll compromise and meet at 4:30.* 2. to bend one's standards *Don't compromise your stand for Christ.*

concerned con cerned (kən sərnd´) adj. interested in, burdened *Tracy is concerned about her aunt's health.*

condition con di tion (kən dish´ ən) n. 1. the ideas upon which an agreement is based *We could not agree to every condition of the contract.* 2. a state of health or being *Dad is in no condition to play football.*

conduct con duct (kon´ dukt) n. behavior *Your conduct has set a good example.* (kən dukt´) v. 1. to lead, guide *The tour guide will conduct us through the building.* 2. to behave *The students always conduct themselves well when they go on a field trip.* 3. to carry *These wires will conduct electricity.*

confession con fes sion (kən fesh´ ən) n. the act of telling the truth or telling about sin *Our confession of sin is a step to salvation.*

conforming con form ing (kən fôrm´ ing) v. becoming similar, molding *Jane is conforming her hairstyle to that of her friends.*

confusion con fu sion (kən fū´ zhən) n. the state of being mixed-up *There was much confusion in the emergency room.*

congratulate con grat u late (kən grach´ ū lāt) v. to express rejoicing with someone who has had success *We sent a telegram to congratulate him.*

connection con nec tion (kə nek´ shən) n. 1. a joining together *The connection between the two pipes burst.* 2. a relationship *I don't understand the connection between the two subjects.*

conservation con ser va tion (kon´ sər vā´ shən) n. careful saving of something *We should all be interested in the conservation of our resources.*

considerate con sid er ate (kən sid´ ər it) adj. thoughtful *Being considerate of older people is important.*

construct con struct (kən strukt´) v. to build *Ricky likes to construct towers with his blocks.*

construction con struc tion (kən strukt´ shən) n. the process of building *The church construction in May.*

continents con ti nents (kont´ ə nənts) n. the large divisions of land on the globe *Europe and Asia are two continents.*

continued con tin ued (kən tin´ ūd) v. kept going; lasted, endured *The game continued into overtime.*

contract con tract (kon´ trakt) n. an agreement between two people or groups, usually in writing *My dad has a contract to build several houses.* (kn trakt) v. 1. to become smaller *Some things contract when they get cold.* 2. to catch an illness *Mr. Bax did not contract malaria on the mission field because he faithfully took his medicine.*

contradict con tra dict (kon trə dikt´) v. to speak in opposition, deny *He will try to contradict what I said.*

convenient con ven ient (kən vēn´ yənt) adj. easy to do, little trouble *It wasn't convenient to shop in the rain.*

conversation con ver sa tion (kon vər sā´ shən) n. 1. talk, oral sharing *Our conversation was interrupted.* 2. conduct *Make sure your conversation honors Christ.*

conversed con versed (kən vərst´) v. talked *The family conversed all evening.*

convertible con vert i ble (kən vər´ tə bəl) adj. able to be changed *Some of the computer parts are convertible from one computer to another.* n. a car with a top which can be folded back *Their new car is a convertible.*

conviction con vic tion (kən vik´ shən) n. 1. a strong belief *You should be able to support every conviction.* 2. the act of finding guilty *The jury arrived at the conviction quickly.*

corps (kôr) n. 1. an organization of people doing the same work *She is part of a work corps to improve the park.* 2. a branch of the armed forces *The Marine Corps helped in the disaster.*

correction cor rec tion (kə rek′ shən) n. 1. the act of making right, change that makes something right *There is a correction in the phone bill.* 2. punishment meant to develop character *Dad's correction at first seemed harsh.*

corruption cor rup tion (kə rup′ shən) n. 1. decay *Our bodies will have no corruption in Heaven.* 2. evil behavior *Corruption is a part of some businesses.*

could've (kood′ əv) cont. could have *He could've done it by himself.*

counters count ers (koun′ tərz) n. 1. people or things which count *The counters show how many people have entered the building.* 2. long boards used for workspace or displaying products *We replaced two kitchen counters.*

countries coun tries (kun′ trēz) n. 1. regions, territories *Some countries have small populations.*

couple cou ple (kup′ əl) n. pair, partners, two things alike *They make a lovely couple.* v. to join together *The train cars couple easily.*

courageous cou ra geous (kə rā′ jəs) adj. brave *The little girl was rescued by her courageous brother.*

courteous cour te ous (kər′ tē əs) adj. mannerly, polite *Aaron was courteous to his grandmother.*

courtroom court room (kȯrt′ rōōm) n. a place where trials and legal hearings are held *Everyone stood when the judge entered the courtroom.*

covenant cov e nant (kuv′ ə nənt) n. a promise that can't be broken *God made a covenant with Abraham.*

creature crea ture (krē′ chər) n. any created being *A small creature crawled along the table.*

crystal crys tal (kris′ təl) n. clear quartz or glass *The crystal on my watch cracked.* adj. like glass, clear *The crystal glassware has a delicate pattern.*

cubes (kūbz) n. 1. three-dimensional figures with six equal sides, each side being a square *We learned how to measure the volume of cubes today.* 2. things shaped like cubes *We ran out of ice cubes.*

curiosity cu ri os i ty (kūr ē os′ ə tē) n. 1. desire to know or learn *His curiosity sometimes gets him into trouble.* 2. strange, unusual *She works in a curiosity shop.*

curved (kərvd) v. bent *The iron rod is curved.* 2. moved in a bending path *The mountain road curved sharply.*

Dd

daily dai ly (dā′ lē) adj. 1. happening, produced, or used every day *It is important to have daily devotions.* 2. relating to every day *Our city has a daily newspaper.*

dairy dair y (der′ ē) n. a place that processes or keeps milk products *The young children visited the dairy.* adj. related to milk products *Butter is a dairy product.*

deacon dea con (dēk′ ən) n. a church officer who helps minister *Mr. Jemison was elected as a deacon.*

debt (det) n. the condition of owing something *We celebrated when the debt was paid off.*

decided de ci ded (di sīd′ id) v. 1. came to a conclusion *They decided to leave in the morning.* 2. ended by one side winning *The game was decided by one point.*

decision de ci sion (di sizh′ ən) n. determination *She made a decision to receive Christ.*

declare de clare (di kler′) v. 1. to state clearly or emphatically *Iran decided to declare war.* 2. to give account of, as at customs *We had to declare the cameras we had purchased in England.*

defect de fect (dē′ fekt) n. a weakness, blemish, or flaw *The vase was without defect.* (də fekt′) v. to leave one's country to join the enemy *The gymnast wanted to defect.*

defector de fec tor (də fek′ tər) n. a person who leaves his country to join the enemy *The ballerina is a defector from the Soviet Union.*

defendant de fend ant (di fen′ dənt) n. the person who has been accused of something *The defendant said he was not guilty.*

defense de fense (di fens′, dē′ fens) n. the act of protecting or guarding *Our team's defense is better than its offense.*

definite def i nite (def′ ə nit) adj. certain, exact *The program will begin at a definite time.*

deformed de formed (di fȯrmd′) adj. changed so as to be ugly or unattractive *Her leg was deformed in the accident.*

defuse de fuse (dē fūz′) v. to remove the starter or power source *The bomb squad was able to defuse the bomb.*

delicate del i cate (del′ i kət) adj. fragile, easily broken or harmed *The vase is delicate.*

delicious de li cious (di lish′ əs) adj. pleasant to the taste *This casserole is delicious.*

deliverance de liv er ance (di liv′ ər əns) n. rescue *The Lord promises us deliverance from sin.*

delivery de liv er y (də liv′ ər ē) n. a handing over of mail or packages *The letter arrived by special delivery.*

denominator de nom i na tor (di nom′ ə nāt′ ər) n. the bottom number of a fraction which tells the number of parts in a whole unit *Compare the denominator to the numerator.*

deportation de por ta tion (dē pȯr tā′ shən) n. the act of forcing a person to leave a country *The officials had deportation papers for the foreign reporter.*

depository de pos i to ry (də poz′ ə tȯr ē) n. a place where things can be kept safely *You could only get into the depository with a key.*

depressed de pressed (di prest′) v. pulled down with bad feelings, lowered in spirit *The bad weather depressed the campers.* adj. felt sad, sorrowful *Her dad was depressed when he lost his job.*

description de scrip tion (di skrip′ shən) n. the act of picturing something in words *They got a description of the stolen car.*

desert des ert (dez′ ərt) n. dry, barren land with little life *The desert is usually dry.* adj. not lived in *They landed on a desert island.* (di zərt′) v. 1. to abandon *God will never desert us.* 2. to leave without permission *If you desert from the army, you will be in serious trouble.*

deserve de serve (di zərv′) v. to be worthy of because of one's qualities *You deserve a reward for your hard work.*

design de sign (di zīn´) v. to draw or set down an idea *Her goal is to design fashions.* n. an idea, pattern, or sketch *The wallpaper design matches the curtains.*

designate des ig nate (dez´ ig nāt) v. to point out, choose, appoint *Coach will designate a pitcher before the game.*

dessert des sert (di zərt´) n. something, usually sweet, served at the end of a meal *We had pie for dessert.*

destroy de stroy (di stroi´) v. to put to an end, ruin *Please don't destroy those books.*

destroyed de stroyed (di stroid´) v. ruined, broken, torn *The store was destroyed by the fire.*

destruction de struc tion (di struk´ shən) n. the process of breaking, tearing, or ruining *The hurricane left miles of destruction in its path.*

details de tails (də tālz´, dē´ tālz) n. items, small parts that make up something *Christopher had all the details about the science project.*

devil dev il (dev´ əl) n. 1. one of Satan's titles *The devil acts like a roaring lion.* 2. a demon *Jesus boldly cast a devil out of the man.* v. to make a food with a hot, spicy seasoning *I am going to devil some eggs for the picnic.*

diamond di a mond (dī´ ə mənd) n. 1. a hard gem made of crystallized carbon *She recently received a diamond ring.* 2. the playing field in baseball *The baseball diamond was built on the school grounds.*

diary di a ry (dī´ ə rē) n. 1. a daily, written account of one's experiences *Jennifer faithfully keeps a diary.* 2. a book for keeping such an account *Anna's diary is locked with a key.*

dictate dic tate (dik´ tāt) v. 1. to say something aloud for someone else to write *The principal likes to dictate his letters.* 2. to command, or give orders *The bank president will dictate a new policy.*

dictator dic ta tor (dik tāt´ ər) n. a person whose every command must be obeyed and who rules harshly *A dictator took over the government.*

dictionaries dic tion ar ies (dik´ shə ner ēz) n. books that contain the words of a language with their definitions and other information *He used three dictionaries for the assignment.*

difference dif fer ence (dif´ ər əns) n. a contrast between two people or things, state of being dissimilar *Jesus Christ makes the difference in me.*

diffuse dif fuse (di´ fūz´) v. to separate and spread out in all directions *The food coloring will diffuse throughout the mixture.*

dining din ing (dīn´ ing) v. eating dinner *My family will be dining out tonight.*

discount dis count (dis´ kount) v. to reduce the price *The department store will discount all their winter merchandise.* n. a reduction in price *You will receive a discount at the checkout.*

discovery dis cov er y (dis kuv´ ər ē) n. the act of finding something *The discovery of gold brought many people to California.*

disposal dis pos al (dis pō´ zəl) n. the act of getting rid of something *The garbage disposal isn't working.*

disrupting dis rupt ing (dis rup´ ting) v. disturbing, breaking into *Your talking is disrupting the class.*

dissatisfied dis sat is fied (dis sat´ is fīd) v. not pleased *We have been dissatisfied with their service.*

distance dis tance (dis´ təns) n. 1. the space between two places or points *We covered a long distance today.* 2. a point far away *We saw a plane off in the distance.*

dividing di vid ing (di vīd´ ing) v. 1. putting into separate parts *We are dividing the money equally.* 2. putting one number into another in math *This page involves dividing by two-digit numbers.*

doubtful doubt ful (dout´ fəl) adj. unclear, not sure *It is doubtful that we will go on the field trip.*

doves (duvz) n. small birds of the pigeon family *Doves are a symbol of peace.*

downstream down stream (doun strēm´) adv. in the direction of a current *The child's sailboat floated downstream.*

druggist drug gist (drug´ ist) n. pharmacist, someone who can fill prescriptions *The druggist advised me about some cough syrup.*

Ee

earnestly ear nest ly (ər´ nist lē) adv. seriously, sincerely *The team worked earnestly to receive a medal.*

easier ea si er (ē´ zē ər) adj. 1. not as difficult *The science test was easier than the history test.* 2. not as harsh or severe *The judge was easier after the man pleaded guilty.*

easily eas i ly (ē´ zə lē) adv. 1. done with little difficulty or effort *Mark easily scored the winning points.* 2. doubtless *She is easily the best singer in the choir.*

echo ech o (ek´ ō) n. a sound which bounces back over and over as it hits surfaces *There is a clear echo in this valley.*

edict e dict (ē´ dikt) n. an official order issued by someone in authority *The king's edict commanded that Christians stop witnessing.*

effect ef fect (ə fekt´) n. result *The penicillin had a quick effect on the infection.* v. to work to cause something to happen or change *Mr. Schindler will effect a change in our lunch schedule.*

effective ef fec tive (ə fek´ tiv) adj. able to produce a change, producing a desired result *The medicine was effective in curing my pneumonia.*

effort ef fort (ef´ ərt) n. 1. energy used to get something done *You need to put forth more effort.* 2. attempt *He made an effort to apologize.*

electric e lec tric (i lek´ trik) adj. powered by a current resulting from the flow of electrons *My dad uses an electric razor.*

employ em ploy (im ploi´) v. 1. to provide with a job that pays wages *The swimming pool will employ high school students this summer.* 2. to use *You will need to employ all your skills to win the soccer match.*

employment em ploy ment (im ploi´ mənt) n. job, occupation *Ed is looking for employment as an engineer.*

empties emp ties (em′ tēz) v. to remove all contents *He empties the trash can each afternoon.*

enforce en force (in fôrs′) v. to see that a law or rule is obeyed *Our police try to enforce the law.*

enjoyable en joy a ble (in joi′ ə bəl) adj. satisfactory, pleasant *I had an enjoyable time playing with my friends.*

entertain en ter tain (en tər tān′) v. 1. amuse, to hold someone's interest *Clowns will entertain the children at the circus.* 2. to have as guests *Mom will entertain six people for lunch.* 3. to allow a thought *He likes to entertain thoughts of becoming a pilot.*

entrance en trance (en′ trəns) n. way of getting in, door *Use the west entrance.*

envelope en ve lope (en′ və lōp, än′ və lōp) n. container for holding letters *Please place the card in the envelope.*

environment en vi ron ment (in vī′ rən mənt) n. 1. surroundings *We can help protect our environment.* 2. the surrounding conditions that influence a person or community *My home is a happy, secure environment.*

equator e qua tor (i kwāt′ ər) n. a great imaginary circle around the earth, halfway between the two poles *The temperatures are hot around the equator.*

equipment e quip ment (i kwip′ mənt) n. supplies, things needed for a certain job *The boys brought the equipment.*

eruption e rup tion (i rup′ shən) n. 1. a burst of lava from a volcano *People have evacuated the village because of the volcano's eruption.* 2. a sudden outburst of emotion *You can expect an eruption of anger when my brother arrives.*

escaped es caped (ə skāpt′) v. got away, broke loose *My pet rabbit escaped from the cage I built.*

essays es says (es′ āz) n. nonfiction articles which give the author's viewpoint *The essays are due next week.*

estimate es ti mate (es′ tə māt) v. to make a guess based on facts *I estimate we will need two gallons of milk.* (es′ tə mit) n. a guess *I need an estimate of the cost.*

Europe Eu rope (ūr′ əp) n. a continent in the Eastern hemisphere between the Atlantic Ocean and Asia *Jenni's family traveled in Europe last summer.*

evaporate e vap o rate (ə vap′ ə rāt) v. 1. to change from solid or liquid to vapor or steam *The water will begin to evaporate when you boil it.* 2. remove moisture *They evaporate water from dried food.* 3. vanish *The threat seemed to evaporate into thin air.*

evidence ev i dence (ev′ ə dəns) n. 1. something brought to trial to help prove innocence or guilt *The officers had enough evidence to arrest the suspect.* 2. anything that proves *There was no evidence of a robbery.*

evil e vil (ē′ vəl) adj. wicked *As sinners, the thoughts of our hearts are only evil.* n. anything wicked or wrong *We don't need to fear evil, for God is with us.*

except ex cept (ek sept′) prep. besides, other than, all but *Everyone has handed in a project, except Tim.*

exchange ex change (iks chānj′) v. to give in return for something else, trade *I had to exchange my blouse for another color.* n. a trade *I made an even exchange on my purchase.* adj. traded *Marnie is an exchange student from Finland.*

excitement ex cite ment (eks sīt′ mənt) n. a stirring up of feelings *Excitement filled the final seconds of the game.*

excuses ex cus es (ik skū′ səz) n. reasons or explanations *Pam always has lots of excuses.* (iks kū zəz) v. relieves from blame, apologizes *His note excuses his absence.*

expect ex pect (ik spekt′) v. to look for as likely to happen *I expect you to complete the assignment on time.*

explanation ex pla na tion (eks plə nā′ shən) n. the act of making something plain, setting forth a clear reason *Mrs. Shafer gave us an explanation about earthquakes.*

exported ex port ed (eks pôr′ təd) v. sent out of one country to another country *Brazil has exported coffee for many years.*

expression ex pres sion (ek spresh′ ən) n. a word, sign, or phrase that represents a feeling *She uses much expression when she talks.*

expressive ex pres sive (ek spres′ iv) adj. full of feeling, outwardly showing feelings *She uses expressive gestures.*

extend ex tend (ik stend′) v. 1. to reach out, stretch out *Extend your hand when you are ready for a prize.* 2. to broaden, get larger *Germany wanted to extend her borders.* 3. to lengthen *They will extend registration for swimming classes two weeks.*

extra ex tra (eks′ trə) adj. more than enough *We had extra food at the party.*

Ff

factory fac to ry (fak′ tə rē) n. a building in which things are manufactured *Ted worked in a factory last summer.*

faint (fānt) adj. 1. being weak, dizzy, lacking strength *Seeing blood makes me feel faint.* 2. cowardly *As Christians, we cannot afford to be faint about our beliefs.* v. to lose consciousness because of a temporary lessening in the supply of blood to the brain *Dr. Fox checked Bryan because he would faint after running hard.*

faithfully faith ful ly (fāth′ fə lē) adv. loyally, regularly *Nancy practices faithfully every day.*

favorite fa vor ite (fā′ vər it, fāv′ rit) adj. best liked *I'm using my favorite baseball for the game.* n. a person who is well liked and may be given special privileges *Lindsay is a favorite with all her teachers.*

fellowship fel low ship (fel′ ō ship) n. 1. a sharing of interests *We enjoy fellowship after the church service.* 2. a group of people with the same interests *The young married couples at church have a fellowship group.* 3. money paid to a student *Foster was on a college fellowship.* v. to share interests *Let's fellowship together.*

fervent fer vent (fər′ vənt) adj. 1. hot, glowing *The coals burned with fervent heat.* 2. showing intense feeling, earnest *The early Christians were fervent in their witness.*

fiercely fierce ly (firs′ lē) adv. 1. wildly, violently, uncontrollably *The hurricane fiercely bombarded the island for several hours.* 2. eagerly, with effort *He worked fiercely to get his degree.*

figure fig ure (fig′ ūr) n. the symbol for a number *She made a figure eight on the ice.* v. to calculate *We measured the room to figure the cost of carpet.*

fined (fīnd) v. punished by a fine *She was fined 25 cents for the late book.*

finish fin ish (fin′ ish) v. 1. to complete, use up *Finish one job before starting another.* 2. produce a desired look or touch *We will finish the table with a gloss.* n. 1. end *Tony was the first one over the finish line.* 2. something used to give a desired look *We used an oak finish on the table.*

forces for ces (fôr′ səz) n. military power, groups of soldiers, sailors *The United States sent forces into China during World War II.* v. pushes, breaks into *The power of dynamite forces the ground to break up.*

foreign for eign (fôr′ in, fär′ ən) adj. 1. outside one's own locality, from another country *Her dad is on the foreign missions board.* 2. not natural, not belonging *Bethany had a foreign object in her eye.*

forests for ests (fôr′ əsts) n. thick growths of trees which cover a large area *National forests are guarded by rangers.*

formal for mal (fôr′ məl) adj. 1. having to do with definite customs and ceremonies *The mayor is planning a formal dinner for the city officials.* 2. designed for wear at a special occasion *We will need to wear formal clothes to the banquet.* n. a lady's evening gown *Sheila is wearing a formal to the concert.*

format for mat (fôr′ mat) n. the arrangement of a program, book, newspaper *The director planned the format for the evening's program.* v. to design or outline *He created the format for the newsletter.*

forth (fôrth) adv. forward, onward *Go forth in God's name.*

forty-four for ty - four (fôr′ tē fôr′) adj. four tens plus four ones *Forty-four students went on the field trip.*

foster fos ter (fôs′ tər) adj. share the care of a family member who is not a member by birth or adoption *They have had many foster children.* v. to encourage, aide *Mrs. Haley tries to foster our feelings of success.*

foul (foul) adj. 1. stinking, filthy *The garbage had a foul odor.* 2. not decent, as language *Do not use foul language.* 3. stormy *The foul weather cancelled the baseball game.* n. in baseball, a ball that is not within the lines of play *The foul ball was nearly a home run.*

foundation foun da tion (foun dā′ shən) n. 1. the base on which something stands *The wise man builds his house on a solid foundation.* 2. an organization that funds worthy causes *The foundation donated several thousand dollars to our school.*

fourth (fôrth) adj. after three others *I was the fourth in line.* n. 1. the one after three others *He came in fourth.* 2. one of four equal parts *I ate a fourth of the pie.*

fowl (foul) n. a bird used as food *Pheasant is a fowl.*

fractions frac tions (frak′ shənz) n. 1. any numbers consisting of a numerator and denominator *We have been adding fractions.* 2. parts or pieces *These items can be bought for fractions of the original costs.*

freckles freck les (frek′ əlz) n. small brown spots on the skin *I have freckles on my nose.*

freeze (frēz) v. become solid or hard at a very cold temperature *The pond will probably freeze soon.* 2. to stay still *The little boy yelled, "Freeze!"*

freight (frāt) n. 1. a means of transporting goods by water, air, or land *The missionaries shipped their goods by a freight service.* 2. cargo, goods which are transported *The freight will arrive at noon.*

frightened fright ened (frīt′ ənd) v. scared, afraid *Sue was frightened by the sudden movement.*

fruitful fruit ful (frōōt′ fəl) adj. 1. fertile, producing much fruit *Our peach tree has been fruitful.* 2. producing results *Our new business has been fruitful.*

furniture fur ni ture (fər′ ni chər) n. things in a room which make it able to be lived in *We are looking for furniture for the living room.*

fusion fu sion (fū′ zhən) n. the putting together of different things *The doctor checked the fusion of Mark's broken bones.*

future fu ture (fū′ chər) n. the time that is yet to come *No one knows the future.*

Gg

general gen er al (jen′ ər əl, jen′ rəl) adj. common, for all *Each town had a general store.* n. an officer in the military *George Washington was a general.*

generous gen er ous (jen′ ər əs) adj. giving freely, unselfish *Here is a generous gift for our church.*

geometry ge om e try (jē om′ ə trē) n. a part of mathematics dealing with points, lines, solids and their characteristics and measurement *My sister will take geometry next year.*

glacier gla cier (glā′ shər) n. a large mass of ice *The large ship struck a glacier.*

global glo bal (glō′ bəl) adj. 1. round, spherical *The earth has a global shape.* 2. worldwide *The western nations are seeking global peace.*

government gov ern ment (guv′ ərn mənt, guv′ ər mənt) n. 1. a system of laws *The United States has a republican form of government.* 2. the people who rule *The government wants to pass a new law.*

grammar gram mar (gram′ ər) n. 1. a part of language which deals with sentence structure *Grammar and literature are sometimes taught together.* 2. a group of rules for speaking or writing a language *Melissa had some trouble with Spanish grammar.* 3. one's own manner of speaking or writing *Ida's grammar is better.*

groceries gro cer ies (grō′ sər ēz) n. the food and other supplies sold by a store *They spent an hour buying groceries for the needy family.*

guard (gärd) v. to protect *It is your job to guard the door.* n. a person or thing that protects *A guard was placed by the door.*

guessed (gest) v. made a judgment without enough knowledge to be certain *He guessed at several answers.*

guest (gest) n. 1. a visitor at another's house *I never had Janet as a guest before.* 2. a paying customer *The guest was angry at the hotel manager.* 3. a person invited to perform *The speaker is a special guest.* adj. for visitors *His room is in the guest house.*

guilty guilt y (gil′ tē) adj. not innocent, deserving blame *The jury found the defendant guilty.*

gymnasium gym na si um (jim nā′ zē əm) n. a building for exercise or sports *Our school is building a new gymnasium.*

Hh

handwriting hand writ ing (hand′ rīt ing) n. 1. writing done by hand *Belshazzar saw the handwriting on the wall.* 2. a style of forming letters *His handwriting is very neat.*

happiness hap pi ness (hap′ ē nes) n. the state of being joyful, glad *Our happiness does not depend on circumstances.*

harbor har bor (här′ bər) n. 1. a place of safety *The church provided a harbor for the poor.* 2. a place for ships to anchor *The ship sailed into the harbor.* v. 1. to protect *Eunice was asked to harbor a family.* 2. to be a place for ships *San Francisco is able to harbor many ships.*

heal (hēl) v. 1. make healthy, cure, to be restored to a healthy condition *The sore needs to heal.* 2. free from trouble *God wants to heal our land of sin.*

heavier heav i er (hev′ ē ər) adj. harder to lift, handle, or bear *This package is heavier than that one.*

heel (hēl) n. 1. the back part of the foot *There is a blister on my heel.* 2. the built-up part of a shoe *I need a new heel.* v. follow closely *Our dog, Missy, has learned to heel.*

height (hīt) n. 1. the highest point *We climbed the height.* 2. climax *I had to go to bed at the height of the story's excitement.* 3. the distance from the bottom to the top, elevation or altitude *They measure Sara's height every year and note it on the chart.*

hijacking hi jack ing (hī′ jak ing) v. taking by force, especially forcing a pilot to fly to an unscheduled place *Metal detectors are used to help prevent hijacking.*

historical his tor i cal (his tòr′ i kəl) adj. having to do with or based on history *Historical facts can help us deal with problems today.*

hoarse (hòrs) adj. sounding harsh or rough, character-ized by a husky voice *Dee became hoarse after cheering for two games.*

homemaker home mak er (hōm′ māk ər) n. a housewife, someone who runs a home *The job of a homemaker is very demanding.*

honesty hon es ty (on′ əs tē) n. truthfulness, trustworthi-ness *Honesty is the best policy.*

honorable hon or a ble (on′ ər ə bəl) adj. worthy of respect, respectable *He received an honorable discharge from the U. S. Army.*

horrible hor ri ble (hòr′ ə bəl) adj. terrible *A skunk has a horrible odor.*

horse (hòrs) n. 1. a domesticated animal with four legs, mane, hoofs, and a tail, used for carrying loads *Jim wants a horse of his own.* 2. a sawing frame *We braced the boat against the wooden horse.* 3. in gymnastics, a piece of equipment used for vaulting *His best gymnastics event is the horse.*

hostage hos tage (hos′ tij) n. someone taken captive and held in exchange for something or someone else *The hostage was released without harm.*

how's (houz) contraction for how is or how has *How's your sister doing?*

Ii

icicle i ci cle (ī′ sik əl) n. a pointed, hanging piece of ice *As it warmed, an icicle fell from the roof.*

ideal i de al (ī dē′ əl) adj. 1. acting as a model *The building served as the ideal for the architecture class.* 2. exactly right *While we were in Florida, the weather was ideal.* n. an idea in its best form, a model *My mom is my ideal.*

imagine i mag ine (i maj′ ən) v. 1. think about and form in the mind *Try to imagine a day at the beach.* 2. suppose, guess *I imagine you had an exciting day yesterday.*

imperfection im per fec tion (im pər fek′ shən) n. a defect, flaw, or blemish *The imperfection was so small, it was not noticeable.*

impolite im po lite (im pə līt′) adj. rude, discourteous *It is impolite to interrupt a conversation.*

importance im por tance (im pòr′ təns) n. value, having influence *The Bible's importance is easily seen.*

imports im ports (im pòrts′) v. brings things into one country from another country *The U. S. imports bananas.* (im′ pòrts) n. things brought into one country from another country *Imports pass through U.S. customs.*

impression im pres sion (im presh′ ən) n. 1. a mark or imprint made by pressing in *She left an impression of her foot in the sand.* 2. the idea, feeling, or effect one has on another *He wants to make a good impression on his boss.*

included in clud ed (in klo͞o′ ded) v. made a part of, involved *She wanted to be included in the plans.*

incorrect in cor rect (in kə rekt′) adj. wrong, improper *He had an incorrect answer.*

incorruptible in cor rupt i ble (in kə rup′ tə bəl) adj. not capable of decay or impurity *We will have an incorruptible body in Heaven.*

increase in crease (in krēs′) v. to grow, multiply *God commanded His creation to increase.* (in′ krēs) n. growth *We have seen an increase in Sunday school attendance.*

indestructible in de struct i ble (in di struk′ tə bəl) adj. not able to be destroyed *The army seemed to be indestructible.*

industrious in dus tri ous (in dus′ trē əs) adj. full of ambition, diligent, wanting to work *Three industrious salesmen sold forty cars.*

industry in dus try (in′ dəs trē) n. a business responsible for manufacturing many of the same type articles *The steel industry in our area has grown rapidly.*

inform in form (in fòrm′) v. to tell about *I will inform the post office about my address change.*

informative in form a tive (in fòr′ mə tiv) adj. full of news or facts *The special program at the museum was very informative.*

157

innocent in no cent (in′ ə sənt) adj. not guilty, blameless *The jury found the defendant innocent.*

instruct in struct (in strukt′) v. to teach *The tour guide wanted to carefully instruct us about the caves.*

instructor in struc tor (in struk′ tər) n. one who teaches *The swimming instructor encouraged all her students.*

intelligence in tel li gence (in tel′ ə jəns) n. 1. ability to learn *His high intelligence was noticeable when he was very young.* 2. people who gather secret information *The British Intelligence uncovered a terrorist plot.*

intended in tend ed (in ten′ dəd) v. had in mind to do, planned *I intended to do my project early.*

intention in ten tion (in ten′ chən) n. a plan, had in mind *My intention was to inform you of a great opportunity.*

interior in ter i or (in tir′ ē ər) adj. within, inner, inland *The interior walls need painting.* n. 1. the inner part of anything, a view of the inside *She is studying interior design.* 2. the domestic affairs of a country *He is in the Department of the Interior.*

international in ter na tion al (in tər nash′ ə nəl) adj. concerning or involving two or more nations *Food for the World is an international organization.*

interruption in ter rup tion (in tə rup′ shən) n. a break in a conversation or service *The knock at the door was an interruption.*

introduction in tro duc tion (in trə duk′ shən) n. 1. the act of presenting something or someone new *His introduction was made at the beginning of the meeting.* 2. preface of a book *The introduction is at the front.*

invention in ven tion (in ven′ chən) n. something new, a new tool or instrument *The invention of the printing press made Bibles more available.*

inventor in ven tor (in ven′ tər) n. a person who thinks up and makes something new *The inventor usually needs hours of work to make an invention.*

irritable ir ri ta ble (ir′ i tə bəl) adj. easily bothered or annoyed *She is usually irritable with her sister.*

issue is sue (ish′ ōō) n. something which is printed and published regularly *We bought the first issue of the magazine.* v. to publish or put forth *They will issue a warrant for the robber's arrest.*

Jj

jewels jew els (jōō′ əlz) n. 1. gems, valuable stones *The crown was full of jewels.* 2. persons or things which are valuable *Good friends are jewels.*

joined (joind) v. brought or fastened together in close contact *All the fifth grade classes joined together for the assembly.*

joint (joint) n. the place where two things or parts come together *The place where my arm and shoulder connect is called a joint.*

journalist jour nal ist (jər′ nəl ist) n. 1. a person who gathers and writes news, a reporter *He is a journalist for the daily paper.* 2. a person who keeps a diary *Each day the journalist writes in her diary.*

judges judg es (juj′ əz) n. 1. people who hear and decide cases in court, in a contest *Several judges were involved in the speech meet.* 2. leaders of Israel after Joshua and before the kings *Deborah was one of the judges of Israel.* 3. Judges - seventh book of the Old Testament *Judges is an historical book.* v. hears and decides cases in court, in a contest *God judges the righteous and unrighteous.*

jury ju ry (joor′ ē) n. a group of people who hear evidence in a case and decide guilt or innocence *The jury quickly arrived at a verdict.*

Kk

kindergarten teacher kin der gar ten tea cher (kin′ dər gär tən tē′ chər) n. a person who works with young children to prepare them for first grade *The kindergarten teacher is a key person in early education.*

kindnesses kind ness es (kīnd′ nəs əz) n. acts which are sympathetic, generous *Your many kindnesses are most appreciated.*

knives (nīvz) n. sharp instruments used for cutting *We sharpened the knives with our new electric sharpener.*

Ll

laughter laugh ter (laf′ tər) n. a sound which shows enjoyment *The laughter could be heard in the next room.*

legal le gal (lē′ gəl) adj. lawful, based on the law *Their legal fees are kept to a minimum.*

legends leg ends (lej′ ənz) n. stories shared and passed down from one generation to another which are accepted as true, but cannot be checked *We read several legends in class.*

liberty lib er ty (lib′ ər tē) n. freedom *Our liberty came at great cost.*

librarian li brar i an (lī brer′ ē ən) n. a person who directs a room or building with a collection of books *Our librarian taught us some library skills.*

lieutenant lieu ten ant (lōō ten′ ənt) n. an officer ranking below captain *The lieutenant was promoted to captain.*

lifeguard life guard (līf gärd) n. a person whose job is to watch beaches, pools, etc. to prevent drowning *Stacie will be a lifeguard this summer.*

linen lin en (lin′ ən) n. 1. cloth made from flax *Her newest dress is made of linen.* 2. pl. tablecloths, napkins, sheets which are made of linen *She washes the linens separately.* adj. made from flax *The paper has some linen content.*

liquid liq uid (lik′ wid) n. a fluid, a substance which flows easily *We added liquid bleach to the laundry.*

liter li ter (lēt′ ər) n. a metric measure of capacity, about the size of a quart *We bought a liter bottle of cola.*

literature lit er a ture (lit′ ər ə chər) n. 1. the writings concerning a specific subject, such as an occupation *Literature on the subject of holidays is easy to find.* 2. writings in prose or verse *Our literature class has been interesting.* 3. printed matter. *We passed out literature concerning the special meetings at church.*

litter lit ter (lit′ ər) n. 1. trash *Litter was everywhere in the park.* 2. a cot for carrying the sick *The paramedics used a litter to lift the victim.* 3. material used as bedding for animals *Change the cat's litter weekly.* 4. the babies born at one time to an animal *Five kittens were in the litter.*

local lo cal (lō′ kəl) adj. about a particular place *We watch the local news every evening.*

loosely loose ly (lōōs′ lē) adv. not tightly, giving room *The dress was loosely fitted.*

loosen loo sen (lōōs′ ən) v. to make less tight *I needed to loosen my belt after Thanksgiving dinner.* 2. unfasten *Loosen the lock on the box.*

losing los ing (lōōz′ ing) v. 1. misplacing *I keep losing my keys.* 2. failing to win *Our team is losing by several points.*

lovingly lov ing ly (luv′ ing lē) adv. in a way which shows devotion or expresses tenderness *Jesus lovingly watches over us all night.*

loyalty loy al ty (loi′ əl tē) n. faithfulness, devotion, support *Citizens should show their loyalty to their country.*

lying ly ing (lī′ ing) v. 1. resting *The dog is lying on the couch.* 2. telling untruthful things *She is lying to you.* adj. false *God hates a lying tongue.*

Mm

machinist ma chin ist (mə shēn′ ist) n. a person who builds and repairs devices with moving parts *The machinist is skilled with his hands.*

magazines mag a zines (mag′ ə zēnz) n. 1. publications usually containing stories, articles, etc. and issued periodically *We used the old magazines to find pictures for the report.* 2. storage places for military supplies, such as gunpowder *The army tried to capture the enemy magazines for additional ammunition.*

major ma jor (mā′ jər) adj. greater in size or importance *We will have a major test next Tuesday.* n. 1. an officer above captain *He is going to be promoted to major.* 2. field of study a student is pursuing *Her major is law.*

manager man ag er (man′ ij ər) n. a person in charge of something, such as a business *My mom was named the new branch manager.*

mantel man tel (man′ təl) n. the shelf projecting from a fireplace *The figurines are on the mantel.*

mantle man tle (man′ təl) n. 1. a cape or cloak *Elisha took up Elijah's mantle.* 2. anything that covers, as snow *The mantle of snow was a beautiful scene.* 3. in geology, the layer of earth between the crust and the core *It is difficult to study the earth's mantle.*

manufacture man u fac ture (man′ yə fak′ chər) v. 1. to make by machinery *We manufacture toasters in this factory.* 2. to make up *He can manufacture excuses easily.*

material ma te ri al (mə tir′ ē əl) n. 1. what a thing is made of *What kind of material are you using for your sculpture?* 2. cloth or fabric *Her dress is a satin material.* adj. 1. having to do with matter *Science deals with material objects.* 2. having to do with pleasure and wealth rather than spiritual values *She has too much focus on material things.*

mathematics math e mat ics (math′ ə mat′ iks) n. a science dealing with numbers and symbols, including arithmetic, algebra, geometry, etc. *Three mathematics courses are required for graduation.*

measuring mea sur ing (mezh′ ər ing) v. finding the size of something *We are measuring the room.* adj. having to do with finding the size *We used all the measuring cups.*

medal med al (med′ əl) n. a piece of metal with writing, given to award some action *He received a medal of honor for military service.*

meddle med dle (med′ əl) v. interfere *Our adviser tries not to meddle with our plans.*

medicine med i cine (med′ ə sən) n. a substance used for healing or pain relief *The pharmacy didn't have the prescribed medicine.*

message mes sage (mes′ ij) n. 1. a communication, usually written or spoken *There is a message for you at the office.* 2. the idea an artist or author is trying to make known *Find the author's message in this book.*

metal met al (met′ əl) n. any of a group of elements, such as iron or copper, which are solid, conduct heat, and can be shaped *The airport has a metal detector.*

midnight mid night (mid′ nīt) n. the middle of the night, twelve o'clock *Paul and Silas prayed at midnight.*

million mil lion (mil′ yən) adj. 1. one thousand times one thousand, 1,000,000 *He hopes to earn a million dollars.* 2. a very large but indefinite amount *We could see a million stars.*

ministry min is try (min′ is trē) n. 1. the act of serving *Each person's ministry should be guided by the Lord.* 2. the office or group of people who are in the office of serving *They have begun a new ministry to provide free medical care.*

minute min ute (min′ it) n. 1. a period of time consisting of sixty seconds *Boil the mixture for one minute.* 2. a short period of time *I will be finished in a minute.* 3. pl. a record of what was done and said at a meeting *We will hear the minutes of the last meeting.* (mī nūt′) adj. 1. very small *She used a magnifying glass to see the minute particles on the glass.* 2. not significant *My problems seem minute compared to his.* 3. exact *Sharon checked everything in minute detail.*

misinformation mis in for ma tion (mis in fȯr mā′ shən) n. wrong facts *Be careful of misinformation.*

mission mis sion (mish′ ən) n. 1. a group of missionaries, their work, or place where they work *They will be leaving soon for the mission.* 2. a job or goal *My mission is to be a good representative for Christ.*

missionaries mis sion ar ies (mish′ ən er ēz) n. people who share the Gospel of Christ, often in a foreign country *Many missionaries are here for our conference.*

motivate mo ti vate (mōt′ ə vāt) v. to provide a stimulation to do something *Alice tried to motivate her brother to help clean the house.*

multiplying mul ti ply ing (mul′ tə plī ing) v. 1. increasing in number *The number of mice is multiplying.* 2. finding the product of two numbers *You will calculate the area by multiplying length times width.*

muscle mus cle (mus′ əl) n. groups of tissues in the body which can contract and expand to cause movement *He pulled a muscle in the game yesterday.*

museum mu se um (mū zē′ əm) n. a building or area in a building in which one finds displays of objects of interest in one or more of the arts or sciences *A museum of natural history is the place to visit for hours of learning.*

musical mu si cal (mū′ zi kəl) adj. 1. having to do with music *The girls played musical chairs.* 2. skilled in music *Their whole family is musical.* n. a theater performance centered around music *The school musical was excellent.*

mysteries mys ter ies (mis′ tə rēz) n. things that have not been or cannot be explained *The class read several mysteries together.*

Nn

naughty naugh ty (nôt′ ē) adj. not behaving *It was naughty of them not to listen to the teacher.*

necessary nec es sar y (nes′ ə ser ē) adj. essential, required, needed *It is necessary to study God's Word.*

neighborly neigh bor ly (nā′ bər lē) adj. friendly *Our friends are neighborly when a new family moves in.*

neither nei ther (nē′ thər, nī′ thər) adj., pron., conj. not either, used with nor *Neither one received the postcards.*

nephew neph ew (nef′ ū) n. the son of a sister or brother *My nephew is in first grade.*

nervous nerv ous (nər′ vəs) adj. 1. showing emotional strain or tension *He has a nervous habit of tapping.* 2. fearful *Miss Deitrich is nervous about her job interview.*

ninth (nīnth) adj. occurring after eight others *I was the ninth person in line.* n. one of nine equal parts *I received a ninth of the votes.*

nonfiction non fic tion (non fik′ shən) n. something told or written that is factual *The Bible is a nonfiction book.*

nonsensical non sen si cal (non sen′ sə kəl) adj. foolish, silly, ridiculous *Several of his poems are nonsensical.*

normal nor mal (nôr′ məl) adj. average, usual *Her temperature is normal.*

noticeable no tice a ble (nōt′ is ə bəl) adj. easily seen, obvious *The drop in temperature was noticeable.*

notion no tion (nō′ shən) n. idea *He has a notion that he can become the star player in baseball.*

novels nov els (nov′ əlz) n. long stories which usually portray imaginary characters and events *Novels are usually fiction.*

numerous nu mer ous (noo′ mər əs) adj. many *There are numerous ways to serve the Lord.*

nutritious nu tri tious (noo trish′ əs) adj. having good value as food *Eating vegetables is nutritious.*

Oo

obedient o be di ent (ō bē′ dē ənt) adj. doing what one is told *Being obedient is part of God's plan.*

obeyed o beyed (ō bād′) v. followed commands or guidance *Moses obeyed the voice of God.*

objection ob jec tion (əb jek′ shən) n. act of disapproving or disagreeing *She has an objection to eating spinach.*

obstruct ob struct (əb strukt′) v. to block, to keep something from taking place as arranged *The new skyscraper will obstruct the view of the city.*

obstruction ob struc tion (əb struk′ shən) n. a blockage, obstacle *Debris created an obstruction in the sewer line.*

obtain ob tain (əb tān′) v. get *Elisabeth was able to obtain a driver's license.*

occurred oc curred (ə kərd′) v. happened *The accident occurred on the way to school.*

oceans o ceans (ō′ shənz) n. large bodies of salt water which cover about three-fourths of the earth *The North American continent touches two oceans.*

o'clock o' clock (ə klok′) adv. of the clock *The service begins at ten o'clock.*

officers of fi cers (ôf′ ə sərz) n. 1. people in positions of authority in business, government, military, etc. *Our club elected new officers.* 2. policemen *Several officers were called to the scene.*

Olympic O lym pic (ō lim′ pik) adj. related to international athletic competition *Eric Liddell was an Olympic runner.*

onions on ions (un′ yənz) n. plants with strong taste and smell, whose edible part grows below ground *The onions added flavor to the stew.*

orbit or bit (ôr′ bit) n. the path a heavenly body takes as it revolves around another heavenly body *Jupiter's orbit is larger than that of Mars.* v. to move in a regular path around something *The earth will orbit around the sun in one year.*

ordinary or din ar y (ôr′ dən er ē) adj. usual, regular, common *The day began in an ordinary way.*

others oth ers (uth′ ərz) pron. everyone else *We want others to follow Christ.*

ought (ôt) v. forced by duty *You ought to see your dentist.*

ourselves our selves (our selvz′) pron. our own selves *We have no one but ourselves to blame for the situation.*

Pp

parachute par a chute (per′ ə shoot) n. a large piece of cloth used when jumping from an airplane *The parachute opened when I pulled the cord.* v. to jump from a plane using a cloth device *The group will parachute in a circular formation.*

parallel par al lel (per′ ə lel) adj. lines, sides, or objects that are an equal distance apart at every point and never meet *A square has pairs of sides which are parallel.*

particular par tic u lar (pər tik′ yə lər, pär tik′ yə lər) adj. 1. certain, specific, definite *Clarence had a particular pair of shoes he wanted.* 2. careful, not satisfied with the ordinary *Tarika is particular about where she shops.* n. facts, details *Do you have all the particulars of the story?*

passports pass ports (pas′ pôrts) n. official documents issued to give permission to travel to other countries *Passports are needed to travel to France.*

pattern pat tern (pat´ ərn) n. 1. a model or form used as a guide *She bought a pattern for the new dress.* 2. a design or arrangement *The pattern in the floor tile must match perfectly.* 3. a regular route *Jim followed the usual flight pattern over the mountains.* v. to shape for a model *If we pattern our lives after Christ's, we will be more content.*

pearls (pərlz) n. 1. hard, white growths which develop around grains of sand in oysters *Her necklace is made of pearls.* 2. anything like a pearl *Her teeth look like pearls after she has been to the dentist.* 3. a strand of pearls *She wore pearls with her black dress.*

percent per cent (pər sent´) adv., adj. per hundred *The bank's interest is at a five percent rate.* n. part of a hundred *Martha got ninety-three percent on her test.*

perfection per fec tion (pər fek´ shən) n. the quality of being without fault or defect *We won't reach perfection until we get to Heaven.*

perfectly per fect ly (pər´ fikt lē) adv. 1. done in a way which is without fault *The drama was performed perfectly.* 2. completely *Her dad was perfectly honest.*

performance per form ance (pər fòr´ məns) n. something done, usually before an audience *There will be a special matinee performance on Saturday.*

performed per formed (pər fòrmd´) v. 1. did something before an audience *Allison performed at the piano recital.* 2. completed, accomplished *Tony performed his job just like the boss expected.*

perfume per fume (pər´ fūm) n. a pleasant odor, scent *Michelle is wearing my favorite perfume.* (pər fūm´) v. to fill the air with a pleasant odor *The air freshener will perfume the room.*

period per i od (pir´ ē əd) n. 1. mark of punctuation at the end of a statement *Don't forget to use a period at the end of your sentence.* 2. era, a segment of time *War is a difficult period of time.* 3. the portion of time into which a game or school day is divided *She has math fifth period.*

phrase (frāz) n. a group of words which helps the sentence meaning, but is not a sentence itself *The prepositional phrase added meaning to the sentence.*

physician phy si cian (fə zish´ ən) n. doctor, someone who practices medicine *A physician has many years of training.*

pier (pir) n. a structure built out over the water as a landing place *The rowboat was tied to the pier.*

plainly plain ly (plān´ lē) adv. 1. clearly, obviously *Jesus is plainly the best friend you'll ever have.* 2. simply *Her story is plainly not true.*

plaintiff plain tiff (plān´ tif) n. person who files a charge in court *The plaintiff is suing her neighbor.*

pneumonia pneu mo nia (noo mōn´ yə) n. an inflammation of the lungs *She developed pneumonia after surgery.*

politician pol i ti cian (pol ə tish´ ən) n. a person involved in government *A politician should listen to the people.*

pollution pol lu tion (pə loo´ shən) n. the state of being impure or soiled *The pollution in the river killed the fish.*

popular pop u lar (pop´ ū lər) adj. well-liked *He is a popular candidate.*

population pop u la tion (pop yə lā´ shən) n. 1. the number of people living in a country or region *The population of the United States is about 250 million.* 2. a group of organisms living in a particular habitat *The swamp has a large population of mosquitoes.*

position po si tion (pə zish´ ən) n. 1. the way in which something is placed *The girl's position was near the door.* 2. a belief taken on a question *Governor Lewis explained his position on education.* 3. social or official rank *Steve's position is quarterback.*

possibility pos si bil i ty (pos ə bil´ ə tē) n. something which may happen *There is a possibility of rain today.*

practical prac ti cal (prak´ ti kəl) adj. useful, sensible *An assignment book is a practical tool.*

practice prac tice (prak´ tis) v. to do over and over in order to improve. *Brent needs to practice an hour every day.* n. 1. a session for doing something repeatedly *Rick has basketball practice today.* 2. a business *Dr. Collier is not ready to sell his practice.*

prayer (prer) n. the practice of talking to God *He whispered a prayer of thanksgiving.*

preacher preach er (prē´ chər) n. a person who tells the Gospel, usually in a church *His goal is to be a preacher.*

precious pre cious (presh´ əs) adj. of great value *A new baby is precious.*

predict pre dict (pri dikt´) v. to tell of a future event, foretell *Many try to predict a date for Christ's return.*

prediction pre dic tion (pri dik´ shən) n. a telling of a future event *A prediction spoken by a false prophet will not come true.*

preferred pre ferred (pri fərd´) v. liked better, put before in one's liking *I preferred chocolate ice cream.*

prejudice prej u dice (prej´ ə dis) n. an opinion formed before all the facts are known *Hitler's prejudice of the Jews resulted in a holocaust.*

prepaid pre paid (prē pād´) v. paid for in advance *The theater tickets were prepaid.*

prepare pre pare (prə per´) v. 1. get ready *She took notes to prepare for her class test.* 2. make or construct according to a plan *I will help my mom prepare dinner.*

preserving pre serv ing (pri zər´ ving) v. keeping safe from harm or decay *I am preserving the peaches.*

pressure pres sure (presh´ ər) n. 1. weight *There was too much pressure on the rope.* 2. influence *When Dad applies pressure, John does better in school.*

pressurized pres sur ized (presh´ ər īzd) v. kept like normal atmospheric pressure *An airplane is pressurized while in flight.*

prevent pre vent (pri vent´) v. to keep from happening *We would like to prevent war.*

previous pre vi ous (prē´ vē əs) adj. occurring before *I made a previous trip here a few years ago.*

private pri vate (prī´ vət) adj. 1. not public *David attends a private school.* 2. belonging to a particular person or group *This whole area is private property.*

process pro cess (pros′ es) n. a step by step method of doing something *The steel making process is complex.* v. to put something through a step by step method *We will process your application.*

produce pro duce (prə dōōs′) v. to make or manufacture *Our company wants to produce more merchandise this year.* (prō′ dōōs) n. 1. something that is made *Our produce will move quickly during the holidays.* 2. vegetables and fruit *The produce is especially fresh in the summer.*

profit prof it (prof it) n. 1. gain *There is no profit in gaining the world, but losing your own soul.* 2. money received from a sale after costs are subtracted *The company made more profit than expected.* v. to benefit *Eric will profit from his father's wise advice.*

proof (prōōf) n. evidence, anything that establishes the truth *The lawyer looked for proof to support his client.*

prophet proph et (prof it) n. 1. a person who speaks for God *Daniel was a prophet for God.* 2. a person who predicts the future *He is a prophet in business matters.*

protection pro tec tion (prə tek′ shən) n. a shielding from danger *The umbrella provided protection from the rain.*

provision pro vi sion (prə vizh′ ən) n. 1. an act or measure taken beforehand *Be sure to make provision for our long trip by bringing plenty to eat.* 2. condition *Under what provision will we be able to accept the treaty?*

published pub lished (pub′ lisht) v. 1. printed for others *The Bible has been published in many languages.* 2. made known, announced *The shepherds published the news that Jesus was born.*

punished pun ished (pun′ isht) v. caused pain or loss because of a wrong *Adam and Eve were punished for their sins.*

purchase pur chase (pər′ chəs) v. 1. to buy *She will purchase a new dress for the party.* 2. to get at great sacrifice *Christ's death was to purchase our salvation.* n. something bought *Take your purchase to the cashier.*

purity pu ri ty (pūr′ ə tē) n. freedom from evil, sin, or contamination *God wants His people to seek purity.*

pursuit pur suit (pər sōōt′) n. 1. a chase *The police were in pursuit of a stolen car.* 2. a career or interest *Computers are his newest pursuit.*

Qq-Rr

raged (rājd) v. 1. showed uncontrolled anger *The patient raged at the nurses.* 2. was violent or uncontrolled *The storm raged for several hours.*

raisin rai sin (rā′ zən) n. a grape dried for food *We ate a raisin salad.*

rare (rer) adj. 1. uncommon *This is a rare book.* 2. unusually excellent *What a rare day this has been!* 3. not well-cooked *He ordered his steak to be cooked rare.*

reasonable rea son a ble (rē′ zən ə bəl) adj. not extreme or unusual *It is reasonable to have a balanced diet.*

reassure re as sure (rē ə shoor′) v. to convince again, to give confidence *He tried to reassure us about the surgery.*

receipt re ceipt (ri sēt′) n. a paper which proves something was received *Bring your receipt to receive a refund.*

received re ceived (ri sēvd′) v. 1. accepted something given *Brian recently received Christ as Savior.* 2. learned, as news *I received a late notice.* 3. greeted, as guests *We were warmly received in the church.*

recently re cent ly (rē′ sənt lē) adv. done at a time just before the present *They recently returned from a cruise.*

reconstruction re con struc tion (rē kən struk′ shən) n. 1. the process of rebuilding *Road reconstruction is scheduled for next summer.* 2. cap. the period of time after the Civil War, when the South was rebuilt *President Johnson had a plan for Reconstruction.*

record rec ord (rek′ ərd) n. 1. an account of events *Our soccer team had a winning record.* 2. anything an account is put on *This is a record of our payments.* 3. a flat disc for playing on a phonograph *The record broke.* re cord (ri kôrd′) v. 1. to make an account of *The weather bureau has to record the temperature daily.* 2. to make an official note *It is her job to record the minutes.* 3. to register sound on a phonograph disc or magnetic tape *He likes to record his voice on tape.*

recount re count (rē kount′) v. to count or number again *He will need to recount the money in the cash register.* n. a second numbering *The candidate is asking for a recount of votes.* (rə kount′) v. to tell the details of *The witness had to recount his story to the jury.*

recycle re cy cle (rē sī′ kəl) v. to use again *We recycle aluminum cans.*

references ref er ences (ref′ ər ən səz) n. 1. remarks referring to something *In the Bible, there are many references to the miracles of Jesus.* 2. signs leading readers to other passages or books *The pastor used many references from the Gospels in his message.* 3. persons to whom inquiries as to character or ability can be made *I need three references for my job application.*

refusal re fus al (ri fū′ zəl) n. the act of saying no *I sent a refusal notice to the magazine.*

refuse ref use (ref′ ūs) n. trash *The gutter was full of refuse.* re fuse (ri fūz′) v. to say no, decline, reject *I had to refuse the invitation.*

refusing re fus ing (ri fūz′ ing) v. saying no, declining, rejecting *He is refusing to eat his supper.*

regiment reg i ment (rej′ ə mənt) n. a military division of two or more battalions *One regiment attacked from the south.*

regions re gions (rē′ jənz) n. 1. parts or areas *There were many dark regions in the stormy sky.* 2. areas of land divided for political or administrative reasons *Mr. Stevens is the company's representative for several regions.*

regular reg u lar (reg′ ū lər) adj. 1. usual, normal *He is able to be on a regular diet.* 2. occurring at set times *The full moon occurs at regular intervals.*

relieve re lieve (rē lēv′) v. 1. to lighten or reduce pain or stress *Aspirin is used to relieve pain.* 2. to free from duty or work *He will relieve me when I go off duty.*

remainder re main der (ri mān′ dər) n. 1. that which is left *The remainder of the meal was placed in containers.* 2. that which is left after dividing one number by another *Every division problem on the page had a remainder.*

repay re pay (rē pā′) v. to pay back *Please repay your debt.*

reporting re port ing (ri pȯrt′ ing) v. 1. giving information about, bringing a message *The newsmen are reporting the latest facts.* 2. appearing, making one's presence known *Steve is reporting for duty.*

rescue res cue (res′ kū) v. to save from danger *Jesus came to rescue us from sin.* n., adj the act of freeing from danger *Mr. Gonzales helped in the rescue attempt.*

resignation res ig na tion (rez ig nā′ shən) n. a formal notice of quitting an office or position, signing again, this time to quit *Mom turned in her resignation yesterday.*

resigned re signed (ri zīnd′) v. to quit an office or position *My dad resigned as director.*

resources re sour ces (rē′ sȯr sez, rə sȯr′ sez) n. 1. available supplies *We have many resources at our fingertips.* 2. wealth *His company resources seem to be unlimited.*

restructured re struc tured (rē struk′ chərd) v. reorganized *The board restructured the firm to create new jobs.*

resupply re sup ply (rē sə plī′)v. to provide something again *We went to the store to resupply the refrigerator.*

reverse re verse (ri vərs′) v. 1. to go backward *She will reverse the numbers to make a puzzle.* 2. to transfer the charges for a phone call *When you call, please reverse the charges.* n. gear in a vehicle or machine which allows it to go backward *Put the car in reverse to go backward.*

revise re vise (ri vīz′) v. to read over and correct as necessary *We had to revise the schedule.*

revision re vi sion (ri vizh′ ən) n. the act or result of correcting *Today's copy is the latest revision.*

revival re viv al (ri vī′ vəl) n. a coming back to life *Our school is experiencing a revival in its devotion to the Lord.*

revive re vive (ri vīv′) v. to bring back to life *They were able to revive her after the accident.*

rhyming rhym ing (rīm′ ing) adj. having the same ending sounds *It was fun to make up rhyming words.*

ridiculous ri dic u lous (ri dik′ yə ləs) adj. so unusual or unreasonable that it is amusing *His suit looks ridiculous.*

righteous right eous (rī′ chəs) adj. without sin, acting the correct way, just *The righteous man loves the Lord.*

ring (ring) v. 1. to give a clear tone when caused to vibrate, to cause a bell to sound *The bell will ring every hour.* 2. to have a sense of humming, as the ears *My ears sometimes ring.* n. 1. the sound of a bell or something similar *We could hear the ring.* 2. a small circular band of metal, often worn on a finger *Her wedding ring is beautiful.* 3. a circular enclosed area for entertainment, as a circus *The lions perform in one ring.* 4. a square bounded by ropes for boxing or wrestling *The boxers perform in a square ring.*

rotation ro ta tion (rō tā′ shən) n. turning around as if on an axis *The earth's rotation causes day and night.*

roughly rough ly (ruf′ lē) adv. 1. harshly, not gently *The prisoner was treated roughly.* 2. about, estimated *We will need roughly eight dozen rolls to feed all the campers.*

royalty roy al ty (roi′ əl tē) n. rank of king or queen *The Queen of England is considered royalty.*

rupture rup ture (rup′ chər) v. explode, break *Sometimes the appendix will rupture.* n. a break, the act of bursting or breaking *When blood vessels rupture, there may be bruises.*

Ss

safety safe ty (sāf′ tē) n. 1. being free from danger *Christ offers us safety from the storms of life.* adj. giving freedom from danger *The car has safety locks in the doors.*

salary sal a ry (sal′ ə rē) n. wage, a fixed amount of pay for services *His salary was increased after two months.*

salesclerk sales clerk (sālz′ klərk) n. a person who sells in a store *She had a job as a salesclerk during Christmas.*

sandwiches sand wich es (sand′ wich əz) n. slices of bread with meat or other filling between the slices *We will serve sandwiches for lunch.*

satisfactory sat is fac to ry (sat′ is fak′ tə rē) adj. good enough, adequate *Her grades are satisfactory.*

saucer sau cer (sô′ sər) n. 1. a shallow dish *Put your cup in the saucer.* 2. anything shaped like a shallow dish *They thought they had seen a flying saucer.*

scientist sci en tist (sī′ ən tist) n. a person who specializes in observing, studying, and experimenting *A scientist must be very orderly and diligent.*

scissors scis sors (siz′ ərz) n. a pair of blades which cross each other so they cut paper or material *These scissors are too dull.*

scratching scratch ing (skrach′ ing) v. 1. scraping with nails to help stop itching *The dog keeps scratching her ears.* 2. cutting slightly *I keep scratching myself on the rose bushes.* 3. stopping, canceling *We ended up scratching most of the committee's ideas.*

sealing seal ing (sēl′ ing) v. 1. closing the contents of something with tape, etc. *He is sealing the box with special tape.* 2. closing tightly, as one's lips *He is sealing his lips to keep the secret.* adj. used for closing *Use sealing tape on the package.*

searching search ing (sərch′ ing) v. 1. exploring, looking for something *Columbus was searching for a route west to Asia.* 2. examining a person for something hidden, as a police officer *The officer was searching the man for a weapon.* 3. looking through writings to find facts *Let's begin searching for the glossary definition.*

security se cu ri ty (sə kūr′ ə tē) n. 1. the state of being free from danger or fear *Christ is our best security for the future.* 2. protection *The national security was threatened.*

selection se lec tion (sə lek′ shən) n. 1. choice *They had a good selection of food.* 2. one who is chosen *The committee's choice for chairman was a good selection.*

seller sel ler (sel′ ər) n. 1. a person who sells, vendor *Lydia was a seller of purple.* 2. something that sells *Hot chocolate is a good seller in winter.*

sense (sens) n. 1. any of the areas capable of receiving messages through nerves and organs *Our sense of sight allows us to see.* 2. a feeling or impression, as warmth *I have a sense of belonging in my family.* 3. the ability to appreciate *Mr. Gold has a good sense of humor.*

sensible sen si ble (sen′ sə bəl) adj. showing good judgment, wise *It is sensible to take an umbrella today.*

sergeant ser geant (sär′ jənt) n. an officer ranking above corporal and below staff sergeant, a police officer below captain or lieutenant *The sergeant was responsible for preparing the men for an emergency.*

serious se ri ous (sir′ ē əs) adj. 1. sober, solemn *A funeral is a serious occasion.* 2. sincere *He was serious when he made that comment.* 3. needing careful thought *I have a serious decision to make.*

services serv ic es (sər′ vi səz) n. 1. meetings held for worship *Sunday services begin at ten o'clock.* 2. armed forces *The armed services include the army and navy.* 3. work done for others, often professional *The dentist offers his services to our teachers at a discount.*

session ses sion (sesh′ ən) n. 1. a meeting, a whole series of meetings *Congress is in a special session.* 2. the time during which a group meets *The session starts at 9:00.*

settlement set tle ment (set′ əl mənt) n. 1. a colony or village *The first settlement was at Plymouth.* 2. an agreement *They made the settlement out of court.*

shelving shelv ing (shel′ ving) n. material used for making lengths of wood for holding things, such as books *There is one hundred feet of shelving in the office.*

shield (shēld) n. 1. a piece of armor carried in the hand *Saul's shield was too large for David.* 2. anything that guards or protects *Our atmosphere acts as a shield.* 3. a metal screen on machinery or artillery *The saw has a safety shield.* v. 1. to protect or guard *His job was to shield the king.* 2. to hide from view *Sunglasses shield my eyes.*

signals sig nals (sig′ nəlz) n. sounds, gestures, etc. which warn or give information *Use hand signals when riding your bike.* v. uses sounds, gestures, etc. to warn or give information *The whistle signals when a train is coming.*

signatures sig na tures (sig′ nə chərz) n. people's names written by themselves *Hundreds of signatures filled the petition.*

sincere sin cere (sin sir′) adj. 1. truthful, without hypocrisy *Bill's testimony was sincere.* 2. real, genuine *Marty showed sincere grief.*

sketch artist sketch art ist (skech′ är′ tist) n. a person who makes quick drawings and designs *A sketch artist laid out the advertisement.*

skiing ski ing (skē′ ing) v. moving over snow or water on two runners or skis *We are going skiing this weekend.*

smother smoth er (smuth′ ər) v. 1. to suffocate, to keep from getting enough air *Be careful not to smother under all those blankets.* 2. cover *Smother the liver in onions.*

social so cial (sō′ shəl) adj. having to do with people living together in groups *Man is a social being.* n. a gathering of people for fun *The church planned a social for the young people.*

soldier sol dier (sōl′ jər) n. 1. a man serving in the army *He became a soldier right after high school.* 2. a person who works hard for a cause *Are you a soldier for Christ?*

solution so lu tion (sə lōō′ shən) n. 1. the answer to a problem *The solution to an addition problem is called the sum.* 2. a mixture of one substance with another *The chemist made a solution in his lab.*

solve (solv) v. to find an answer to a problem *I was able to solve the problem by bringing more desks into the room.*

sorrowful sor row ful (sär′ ə fəl) adj. full of sadness *The funeral was a sorrowful occasion.*

source (sȯrs) n. 1. starting point of a river *The source of a river is usually in the mountains.* 2. the origin of something *We were unable to identify the source of the rumor.* 3. supplier *Cattle are a major source of meat.*

sponge (spunj) n. 1. a sea animal with many pores *We found a sponge which had washed up on shore.* 2. anything with lots of pores *We need a new sponge to wash the boards.*

squares (squerz) n. 1. figures with four equal sides and four equal angles *The table cloths were squares of material.* 2. drawing instruments with two sides which come together at a right angle *A carpenter uses squares to make sure his corners are right angles.* 3. products of numbers multiplied by themselves *We learned how to find squares in math.* v. multiplying numbers by themselves *If he squares the numbers, he will have the right answers.*

squirrel squir rel (squər′ əl) n. a small rodent with a long bushy tail *There was a squirrel in the tree.*

stacks (staks) n. 1. orderly piles of objects *There are stacks of trays at the cafeteria.* 2. the part of a library in which books are stored in racks *You will find the reference books in the library in the front part of the stacks.*

standard stan dard (stan′ dərd) n. 1. a principle or measure with which other things are compared *The Bible is our standard.* 2. a level of excellence *Our country has a high standard of living.* 3. an object used as a symbol *The men carried the standard into battle.* adj. that which is usual, not extra *This standard ruler will be used in mathematics.*

straighten straight en (strāt′ ən) v. 1. unbend *It is easier to straighten the iron rod when it is hot.* 2. to make neat *Straighten your room before inviting your friends over.*

strict (strikt) adj. strongly enforcing rules, closely disciplined *A military school is known for strict discipline.*

structure struc ture (struk′ chər) n. 1. something that is built *This structure was built in 1906.* 2. the way something is put together, such as a business or organization *The company's structure has changed since a new vice-president was selected.* v. to organize *We will structure our program similar to the one at church.*

students stu dents (stōō′ dənts) n. those who attend school or college *Twenty-five students are in the class.*

studied stud ied (stud′ ēd) v. 1. applied the mind to learn *Sam studied history for an hour.* 2. examined closely and carefully *The expert studied the gem.* 3. took a course at college *She studied law enforcement.*

submitting sub mit ting (səb mit′ ing) v. yielding, coming under authority *Submitting to authority is important no matter how old you are.*

substantial sub stan tial (səb stan′ chəl) adj. 1. large *Ben received a substantial raise.* 2. real *The police are looking for something substantial to make an arrest.*

sugary sug ar y (shoog′ ər ē) adj. sweet *The cookie has a sugary taste.*

suggest sug gest (səg jest′) v. to put a thought or idea into the mind *I suggest you comb your hair before leaving.*

suggestion sug ges tion (səg jes′ chən) n. idea, the process by which one thought leads to another *I placed my suggestion in the box.*

suite (swēt) n. 1. a group of rooms *The couple was given the bridal suite.* 2. an early form of instrumental music *We listened to a suite by an early composer.*

superior su pe ri or (sə pir′ ē ər) adj. 1. higher in place or rank *The general is a superior officer.* 2. better in quality or value, above average *We pay more for superior quality.* 3. acting better than others *She acts so superior.* n. a person higher in rank *You must answer to your superior.*

supersonic su per son ic (soo pər son′ ik) adj. above the speed of sound *The missile reached supersonic speeds.*

supervisor su per vi sor (soo′ pər vī zər) n. one who oversees another *My supervisor stopped by unexpectedly.*

suppress sup press (sə pres′) v. to pull under or hold down something *The police tried to suppress the crowd.*

supreme su preme (sə prēm′, soo prēm′) adj. highest rank or authority, best *God is supreme ruler of Creation.*

survey sur vey (sər′ vā) n. a careful examination to learn certain facts *We took a survey of the neighborhood.* (sər vā′) v. to examine carefully *We will survey the area for information about the missing child.*

survival sur viv al (sər vī′ vəl) n. the act of living through an event *Our survival is dependent on food and water.*

survivor sur vi vor (sər vī′ vər) n. one who continues to live after an event or someone else's death *She was the only survivor of the accident.*

sweet (swēt) adj. 1. tasting like sugar *The candy was too sweet.* 2. agreeable, pleasant *She has a sweet spirit.*

sympathy sym pa thy (sim′ pə thē) n. compassion, feeling the way another does *Sympathy is a virtue.*

symptom symp tom (simp′ təm) n. a sign, especially of an illness *A fever is a symptom of many illnesses.*

systems sys tems (sis′ təmz) n. a group of related things *Our body systems are very complex.*

Tt

tabernacle tab er nac le (tab′ ər nak əl) n. 1. a portable sanctuary used by the Israelites in the wilderness *God gave precise instructions for the use of the tabernacle.* 2. a place of worship, church building *The new tabernacle will seat five thousand.*

telegram tel e gram (tel′ ə gram) n. a message sent by means of electric impulses carried through wire or radio waves *I received a telegram on my birthday.*

televise tel e vise (tel′ ə vīz) v. to send a far distance to be seen *They will televise most of the championship games.*

televisions tel e vi sions (tel′ ə vizh ənz) n. instruments for receiving signals which allow a picture or image to appear *Most people have color televisions.*

tendency ten den cy (ten′ dən sē) n. a leaning toward, liking *Many have a tendency to take their freedoms for granted.*

terrific ter rif ic (tə rif ik) adj. 1. wonderful, great *We had a terrific time.* 2. causing fear *A terrific wind blew against the house.*

territory ter ri to ry (ter′ ə tȯr ē) n. 1. the land and water under a nation's authority *The Allies invaded enemy territory.* 2. region *This territory was settled long ago.* 3. land under a nation's jurisdiction but without full status *Five states were made from the Northwest Territory.*

therefore there fore (ther′ fȯr) conj. because of, as a result of *We have a large group; therefore, we will meet in the auditorium.*

transformation trans for ma tion (trans fər mā′ shən) n. the process of changing from one thing to another *It was exciting to see the transformation of our building from framework to church.*

transformed trans formed (trans fȯrmd′) v. changed from one thing to another *Our lives are transformed when we receive Christ.*

transfusion trans fu sion (trans fū′ zhən) n. the process of transferring blood from one person to another *My uncle needed a blood transfusion.*

transport trans port (trans pȯrt′) v. to carry from one place to another *They will begin to transport the space shuttle here tomorrow.* (trans′ pȯrt) n. the means or process of carrying from one place to another *A transport carries the space shuttle to the launchpad.*

transportable trans port a ble (trans pȯrt′ ə bəl) adj. able to be carried from one place to another *The luggage is light and transportable.*

transportation trans por ta tion (trans pər tā′ shən) n. a means of carrying or traveling from one place to another *Flying is an expensive means of transportation.*

transporting trans port ing (trans pȯrt′ ing) v. carrying from one place to another *They will be transporting all the soldiers on an army aircraft.*

travel agent trav el a gent (trav′ əl ā′ jənt) n. a person who makes arrangements for tourists or others who go from place to place *As a travel agent, she has had many opportunities to fly.*

treasury treas ur y (trezh′ ər ē) n. a place where valuables or money are kept *The club treasury has ten dollars.* 2. a department in charge of money *My uncle Jerry works at the United States Treasury.*

tremendous tre men dous (tri men′ dəs) adj. very large, wonderful *There was a tremendous revival at school.*

trial tri al (trī′ əl) n. 1. the testing of a case in court *The trial begins Monday.* 2. temptation, time of testing *A trial can test your faith.*

troops (trōops) n. 1. groups of people or animals *The scouts entered the camp in troops.* 2. soldiers *Iraqi troops invaded Kuwait.*

troublesome trou ble some (trub′ əl səm) adj. bothersome, causing irritation *My brother can be troublesome.*

truly tru ly (trōo′ lē) adv. 1. really, actually *Jesus truly was the Son of God.* 2. sincerely *I truly believe in Christ.*

trustworthy trust wor thy (trust′ wər thē) adj. reliable, worthy of trust *He is a trustworthy lawyer.*

typist typ ist (tīp′ ist) n. a person who uses a typewriter *Mrs. Wambold is a fast, accurate typist.*

Uu

umbrella um brel la (əm brel′ ə) n. a shade of cloth over a wire frame used to protect from rain or sun *Don't forget to take an umbrella.*

unbelief un belief (ən bə lēf′) n. lack of belief, especially in religion *His unbelief kept him from accepting Christ.*

uncertain un cer tain (ən sər′ tən) adj. 1. not sure *The date for our next meeting is uncertain.* 2. not reliable *This spring weather is uncertain.*

unexplained un ex plained (ən ek splānd′) adj. not able to be understood, unsolved *She was tardy for some unexplained reason.*

universe u ni verse (ū′ nə vərs) n. all of creation *The universe is so large, we cannot comprehend it.*

university u ni ver si ty (ū′ nə vər′ sə tē) n. a place which offers instruction beyond the high school level, usually having several kinds of degree offerings *The state university offers a degree in agriculture.*

unlikely un like ly (ən līk′ lē) adj. not likely, adv. improbably *It is unlikely to snow here in June.*

Vv

vain (vān) adj. 1. useless, of no value *The toddler tried in vain to reach the candy dish.* 2. conceited *It seems vain to be constantly looking in a mirror.*

value val ue (val′ ū) n. 1. fair price *The cost of the item represented its true value.* 2. the worth of something *The value of the dollar has fallen.* v. 1. to set a price *I value the house at $95,000.* 2. to think highly of *We value our friends very much.*

valuable val u a ble (val′ ū ə bəl, val′ ū bəl) adj. 1. having worth or value *This report is valuable.* 2. of great value, costly *Valuable jewels covered the box.*

vane (vān) n. a piece of wood, metal, or cloth, set up high to show wind direction *The vane indicated a north wind.*

vein (vān) n. 1. a blood vessel that carries blood from the body to the heart *A vein carries blood to the heart.* 2. any of the vessels in a leaf *A vein in a leaf carries nutrients.*

verb (vərb) n. a word which shows action or state of being *Every sentence must have a verb.*

verbal ver bal (vər′ bəl) adj. having to do with words, oral, not written *We have a verbal agreement with the mechanic.*

verses ver ses (vər′ səz) n. 1. stanzas, lines, or sections of a poem or song *We sang three verses.* 2. divisions of a chapter in the Bible *We read several verses from Psalms.*

version ver sion (vər′ zhən) n. 1. a translation of the Bible *He used the King James Version.* 2. one point of view *The judge wanted to hear my version of the accident.*

video tape vid e o tape (vid′ ē ō tāp′) n. a magnetic strip on which impulses can be recorded for later viewing *The video tape has several cartoons on it.*

view (vū) n. 1. sight, vision *No one was in view.* 2. a scene *The view of the mountain was wonderful.* 3. opinion *Her view on education is interesting.* v. to inspect, look at *Let's view the film again.*

visibility vis i bil i ty (viz′ ə bil′ ə tē) n. the farthest distance at which something can be seen *The fog made the visibility near zero.*

visible vis i ble (viz′ ə bəl) adj. able to be seen *There has been visible improvement in her condition since yesterday.*

vision vi sion (vizh′ ən) n. 1. a dream *Daniel had a vision.* 2. sight *My sister needs to have her vision checked.*

visitors vis i tors (viz′ ə tərz) n. people who come as guests *Our visitors are made to feel welcome at church.*

visors vi sors (vī′ zərz) n. parts which are fastened to something to protect or shade the eyes *Visors help keep the sun out of my eyes.*

visual vis u al (vizh′ ū əl) adj. concerned with seeing *You use visual clues when you try to describe something.* n. something used to help picture an explanation *He used a visual in his presentation for chapel.*

vital vi tal (vī′ təl) adj. 1. needed for life *Vitamins are vital for good health.* 2. necessary *A dentist's equipment is vital for efficient service.*

vitality vi tal i ty (vī tal′ ə tē) n. energy *His vitality seems to be endless.*

vitamins vi ta mins (vīt′ ə minz) n. nutrients found in most foods and essential for good health *Vitamins help the body grow and function.*

vivid viv id (viv′ id) adj. 1. full of life *She has a vivid personality.* 2. bright, colorful *As an artist, he is known for using vivid colors.*

volleyball vol ley ball (vol′ ē bôl) n. a game played by hitting a large inflated ball over a net *The girls won the volleyball match.*

volumes vol umes (vol′ ūmz) n. 1. books *Our library has over one thousand volumes.* 2. two or more of a series of books forming a complete work or collection *My encyclopedia has twenty volumes.*

Ww

wearing wear ing (wer′ ing) v. 1. having on the body *He is wearing a ski jacket.* 2. tiring *The constant noise is wearing on my nerves.* 3. becoming useless, as wearing out *The living room furniture is wearing out fast.*

weary wea ry (wir′ ē) adj. 1. tired *Jeff was weary after walking two miles.* 2. impatient *God never gets weary of our prayers.*

weighed (wād) v. 1. measured the amount of heaviness *He weighed himself before he ate breakfast.* 2. measured out *The cook weighed equal portions of sugar and flour.* 3. considered or pondered *The judge weighed both points of view.* 4. burdened *We are all weighed down with a burden of sin before we are forgiven.*

weird (wird) adj. 1. strange, mysterious, odd *Our dog acts weird when she hears the doorbell.*

whether wheth er (weth′ ər) conj. 1. if it might be *Miss Smart asked whether she might be able to help with the party.* 2. in either situation *I know whether he walks or rides his bike, he'll be here on time.*

whisper whis per (whis′ pər) v. 1. to speak very softly *Please whisper in the library.* 2. to make a soft, rustling sound *I could hear the leaves whisper in the breeze.*

wholesale whole sale (hōl′ sāl) n. the selling of goods in large quantities at lower prices *We bought our office supplies wholesale.* adj. relating to lower prices *Their wholesale prices attract many customers.*

workmanship work man ship (wərk′ mən ship) n. 1. skill *Garrett was proud of his workmanship when he finished his project.* 2. something made using a skill *We are God's workmanship.*

worst (wərst) adj. most bad, most unpleasant adv. most badly *That is the worst music I have ever heard!*

would've would 've (wood′ əv) cont. would have *We would've been on time, but we were caught in traffic.*

wound (wound) v. 1. turned, or made to revolve *He wound the watch every day.* 2. to turn around something so as to form a ball *The thread wound on a spindle.* (wōōnd) n. an injury *The soldier's wound was not serious.* v. to injure *Don't wound his spirit.*

wring (ring) v. 1. to squeeze or twist to force out liquid *You will need to wring out the sponge when you mop the floor.* 2. to twist the hands together in distress *She tends to wring her hands when she is worried.*

Xx-Yy-Zz

yearn (yərn) v. desire, filled with longing *Christians yearn for their heavenly home.*

you've (yōōv) cont. you have *Tell me if you've found my coat.*

youthfulness youth ful ness (yōōth′ fəl nes) n. the quality of being young, full of life and energy *Youthfulness is an advantage in many situations.*

5th Grade Word Bank

Home Base and Personal Words

_____
_____
_____
_____
_____
_____
_____
_____
_____
_____
_____
_____
_____
_____
_____
_____
_____
_____
_____
_____
_____
_____
_____
_____
_____

Aa
a
able
about
above
abruptly
absence
absent
accept
accident
account
accountable
accountant
accuse
accustom
achieve
across
action
active
actor
add
addition
address
adjective
admire
adoption
adulthood
advantage
adventure
advice
advisable
advise
advisory
affect
affected
affection
afford
afraid
African
after
afternoon
afterwards
again
against
aggravate
agree
agreement
airplane
airport
alike
alive
all
all right
alley
allow
almighty
almost
along
aloud
already
also

altar
alter
alternate
although
always
am
America
American
among
amount
amusement
an
anchor
and
angel
angels
angles
animals
ankle
annoy
anoint
anonymous
another
answer
answered
answering
any
anybody
anyone
anything
anyway
anywhere
apartment
apparent
appear
apple
appreciate
April
arctic
are
area
aren't
argue
arithmetic
arms
around
arrange
arrive
arrow
as
Asian
asked
asking
assemble
assembly
assignment
assistant
associate
astronaut
at
ate

athlete
atmosphere
attempt
attend
attendant
attention
attentive
attic
attorney
August
aunt
aunt's
authority
authors
autograph
automatic
automotive
autumn
avenue
average
aware
away
awesome
awful
awfully
awhile

Bb
baby
back
backache
bacon
badge
balance
ball
balloons
balm
banana
banker
banquet
baptize
bare
bargain
baseball
basketball
bass
be
beaches
bear
beat
beautiful
beauty
became
because
becoming
bed
bedroom
bedspread
beehive
been
before

began
begin
beginning
behave
behind
beige
belief
believe
believes
bell
below
benches
beneath
beneficial
berries
betrayal
better
between
Bible
biblical
bicycle
big
biggest
bike
billfold
billion
binders
biographies
birthday
birthright
biscuit
bite
black
blanket
bless
blind
blindness
blood
bloody
blue
body
books
bookshelf
borrow
bosses
both
bother
bottom
bought
bound
bowl
box
boxes
boy
boyfriend
brain
brake
branches
bread
break
breakable

breakfast
breath
breathe
bridges
bright
brighter
brightest
bring
bringing
broad
broil
broken
brook
brother
brothers
brought
brown
browse
bruised
buckle
bug
bugle
build
builder
built
bundle
buried
burst
bushel
business
businessman
busy
but
butterfly
button
buy
buying

Cc
cabin
cabinet
cages
cake
calculate
calculator
calendar
calendars
calling
calming
calmly
calves
came
can
can't
candle
candy
cannot
canoe
captain
car
cardboard

_____
_____
_____
_____
_____
_____
_____
_____
_____
_____
_____
_____
_____
_____
_____
_____
_____
_____
_____
_____
_____
_____
_____
_____
_____
_____
_____
_____
_____
_____
_____
_____

care	circus	condition	cross	deportation
careful	cities	conduct	crosswalk	depository
carefully	citizens	confess	crowd	depressed
careless	claimed	confession	crown	description
carols	clasp	conforming	crucial	desert
carry	class	confused	crucify	deserve
carrying	classes	confusion	crumbs	design
cartoons	cleaned	congratulate	crystal	designate
castles	clearly	connect	cubes	desks
cat	climate	connection	cucumber	dessert
catalog	climbed	conservation	cuddle	destroy
catastrophe	clock	considerate	curiosity	destroyed
catcher	close	Constitution	curious	destruction
catsup	closet	construct	current	details
cattle	clothes	construction	curtain	devil
caught	clothing	contain	curve	devotions
caused	cloudy	contend	curved	diamond
ceiling	clowns	contest	cushion	diary
celebration	coach	continents	cut	dictate
cellar	coach's	continued	cute	dictator
center	coast	contract		diction
central	coat	contradict	**Dd**	dictionaries
century	cocoa	control	daily	dictionary
cereal	coconut	convenient	dairy	did
certainly	coffee	conversation	damage	didn't
chair	coins	conversed	danger	difference
chalkboard	cold	convertible	dangerous	different
chances	collar	conviction	daughter	differently
changing	collect	cookies	day	diffuse
chapter	collection	copies	days	digestion
charged	colonel	corner	deacon	dining
check	color	corps	deaf	dinner
checkout	colorful	correct	dear	dinosaur
checkers	column	correction	dearest	direction
cheerful	combine	corruption	death	dirty
cheese	combing	cost	debt	disappear
cherish	come	cough	deceive	disappoint
chest	comfort	could	December	disciple
chief	comfortable	could've	decided	discipline
chiefly	comics	couldn't	decision	discount
child	coming	count	declare	discover
children	command	counters	dedication	discovery
children's	commander	countries	deer	disease
chillier	in chief	country	defect	dishonest
chilly	commandment	countryside	defective	disliked
chimney	comment	couple	defector	dismissed
Chinese	commercial	courage	defendant	disobey
chips	common	courageous	defense	display
chocolate	company	court	definite	disposal
choice	compare	courteous	deformed	disrupting
choices	compassion	courthouse	defuse	dissatisfied
choir	complain	courtroom	delay	distance
choose	complaining	cousins	delicate	distrust
choosing	complaint	covenant	delicious	dive
chores	complete	covered	delighted	divide
chosen	compliment	cowboys	deliverance	dividing
Christ	compound	craft	delivery	divine
Christian	comprehension	creation	denominator	division
Christmas	compress	creature	dentist	do
church	compromise	cries	deny	doctor
circle	concerned	crops	dependable	dodge

Home Base and
Personal Words

_____

_____

_____

_____

_____

_____

_____

_____

_____

_____

_____

_____

_____

_____

_____

_____

_____

_____

_____

_____

_____

_____

_____

_____

_____

_____

_____

_____

_____

_____

doesn't	either	expression	fix	fuss
dog	elastic	expressive	fixing	future
doing	electric	extend	flags	
dollars	elephant	extension	flashlight	**Gg**
dolls	eleven	extra	flavor	gallons
don't	eleventh	eyelids	flew	games
done	emotions		flood	garden
door	employ		floor	gasoline
doorknob	employment	**Ff**	flour	gather
double	empties	face	flower	gave
doubtful	encourage	factory	fly	geese
doughnut	encyclopedia	facts	folklore	general
doves	end	faint	following	generous
down	enemies	fairly	food	gentleness
downstairs	enforce	faith	foolish	geography
downstream	engaged	faithful	football	geometry
downtown	engine	faithfully	for	get
dozen	engineer	fall	forces	getting
dozens	enjoyable	false	foreign	giant
dragonflies	enjoyed	families	forest	gifts
draw	enjoyment	famous	forests	gigantic
drawers	enough	fantastic	forever	giggle
drawing	entering	farther	forgetful	girl
dream	entertain	fast	forgive	girl's
dress	entrance	father	forgiving	give
drew	envelope	fault	forgotten	glacier
drill	environment	favor	formal	glad
drink	equator	favorite	format	glasses
drive	equipment	fear	forth	global
druggist	error	fearful	forty-four	gloves
dry	eruption	feasting	forward	gnaw
duck	escape	February	foster	go
during	escaped	feel	fought	God
duty	essays	feeling	foul	goes
dwell	estimate	feet	found	going
	eternal	fellowship	foundation	golden
Ee	Europe	felt	fountain	golf
each	evaporate	fence	four	gone
eager	Eve	fervent	fourth	good
eagle	even	feverish	fractions	good-bye
earlier	evening	fewer	freckles	Gospel
early	everlasting	fields	freedom	got
earned	every	fierce	freeze	government
earnestly	everybody	fiercely	freight	governor
ears	everyone	fifteenth	Friday	gown
earth	evidence	fifth	friend	graceful
easier	evil	fighting	friendly	gracious
easily	example	figure	friendships	grade
easy	excellent	final	fright	grammar
eats	except	finding	frightened	grandfather
echo	exchange	fine	from	grandmother
edge	excitement	fined	front	grandparents
edict	exciting	finger	frozen	graph
education	excuses	finish	fruit	grateful
effect	exercise	fire	fruitful	gray
effective	exited	firefighter	fudge	great
effort	expect	fireplace	fulfillment	green
eggs	explain	firmly	full	groan
eight	explanation	first	fun	groceries
eighth	explore	fish	furniture	gross
eighty	exported	five	fusion	group

170

Home Base and Personal Words

_____
_____
_____
_____
_____
_____
_____
_____
_____
_____
_____
_____
_____
_____
_____
_____
_____
_____
_____
_____
_____
_____
_____
_____
_____
_____
_____
_____
_____
_____
_____

grow
grown
guard
guess
guessed
guesswork
guest
guide
guilty
gym
gymnasium
gymnastics

Hh
had
half
halfway
hall
hamburger
hand
handkerchief
handlebars
handles
handsome
handwriting
hanging
happened
happens
happier
happiness
happy
harbor
hard
has
hasn't
haul
have
haven't
having
hawk
head
headache
heal
health
hear
heard
heart
Heaven
heavier
heavy
height
held
hello
helpful
helpless
here
hero
heroes
herself
hides
high

highest
highway
hijacking
hike
hill
him
himself
historical
hoarse
holiday
Holy
home
homemaker
honesty
honey
honorable
hope
hoping
hopping
horrible
horseback
horses
hospital
hospitals
hostage
hostess
hotel
hour
household
houses
how
how much
how's
however
huge
human
humble
humility
hundred
hung
hungry
hurried
hurry
hurting
hymns

Ii
I
I'd
I'll
I'm
ice cream
icicle
idea
ideal
if
imagine
imperfect
imperfection
impolite
importance

important
imports
impossible
impress
impression
improve
in
inch
included
incorrect
incorruptible
increase
independent
indestructible
Indian
industrious
industry
infection
inform
information
informative
inherit
innocent
insects
inside
instead
instruct
instructor
intelligence
intended
intention
interest
interesting
interior
international
interruption
into
introduction
invention
inventor
invisible
invitation
invite
irritable
is
issue
it
it'll
it's
itching
its

Jj
jacket
January
jaw
jeans
Jesus
jewels
join
joined

joint
journal
journalist
joyfully
judge
judges
July
jumped
June
jungle
jury
just
justice

Kk
keep
keyboard
keys
kick
kind
kindergarten
kindness
king
kingdom
kiss
kitchen
kitten
knee
knelt
knew
knife
knives
knock
know
knowledge

Ll
labeled
laborers
ladies
lady
laid
lake
lamb
language
largest
last
late
later
laugh
laughing
laughter
laundry
laws
lawyer
lazily
laziness
leaf
league
learn
least

leather
leave
led
left
left-hand
legal
legends
legs
lemonade
lessons
let
letters
level
liberty
librarian
library
lies
lieutenant
life
lifeguard
lifts
lightning
like
likes
limb
linen
lion
liquid
listen
liter
literature
litter
little
live
lives
living
loaves
local
location
lonely
long
look
loose
loosely
loosen
Lord
lose
losing
loss
lost
lotion
loudest
love
loving
lovingly
loyal
loyalty
lunchroom
lying

_____
_____
_____
_____
_____
_____
_____
_____
_____
_____
_____
_____
_____
_____
_____
_____
_____
_____
_____
_____
_____
_____
_____
_____
_____
_____
_____
_____
_____
_____
_____
_____
_____
_____
_____
_____
_____
_____
_____
_____
_____
_____
_____
_____

Mm
machine
machinist
made
magazine
magazines
maintain
major
making
mall
man
manage
manager
mantel
mantle
manufacture
many
March
market
married
master
matches
material
mathematics
maybe
me
mean
meant
measure
measuring
meat
mechanic
medal
meddle
medical
medicine
meeting
melted
men
merciful
merrily
mess
message
met
metal
microscope
microwave
middle
midnight
might
might've
mighty
mild
milk
milkshake
million
mind
ministry
minute
miracle
miraculous

mirror
misinformation
misplaced
miss
missed
mission
missionaries
mistake
mistaken
misunderstanding
mix-up
model
mom
Monday
money
monkey
months
more
morning
morning star
mostly
motel
mother
motion
motivate
motorcycle
mountain
mouse
mouth
move
movement
movies
moving
Mr.
Mrs.
much
mud
multiplication
multiplying
muscle
museum
music
musical
musician
must
my
myself
mysteries

Nn
name
narrow
nation
nature
naughty
nearly
necessary
neck
need
needless
neighbor

neighborhood
neighborly
neither
nephew
nervous
new
newspaper
nice
nicest
nickel
niece
nine
nineteen
ninetieth
ninth
no
none
nonfiction
nonsense
nonsensical
noon
normal
north
nose
not
note
nothing
notice
noticeable
notion
noun
novels
November
now
number
numerous
nurse
nutritious

Oo
o'clock
obedient
obeyed
object
objection
obstruct
obstruction
obtain
occurred
ocean
oceans
October
of
off
offerings
officers
offices
often
oil
ointment
old

Olympic
on
once
one
onions
only
open
opening
orange
orbit
ordinary
Oriental
other
others
ought
ounce
our
ourselves
out
outdoors
outfield
outside
outstanding
over
overcome
owner
oxygen

Pp
package
packs
pages
paid
pair
palace
palm
paper
parachute
paragraph
parallel
paramedic
pardoned
parents
parking
particular
parties
party
passes
Passover
passports
pastor
pasture
pattern
peace
peaceful
pearls
pencil
people
percent
perfect
perfection

perfectly
performance
performed
perfume
perhaps
period
permission
person
personal
pet
phrase
physician
pianist
pick
pickle
picnic
picture
pie
piece
pieces
pier
pillow
pink
pioneer
pitcher
pizza
place
plainly
plaintiff
plants
plastic
plate
play
played
playground
playing
pleasant
please
pleasing
pleasure
plus
pneumonia
poetry
point
poison
policeman
politely
politician
pollution
poor
popular
population
portable
position
possibility
post
potatoes
pounds
pouring
power
powerless

_____

_____

_____

_____

_____

_____

_____

_____

_____

_____

_____

_____

_____

_____

_____

_____

_____

_____

_____

_____

_____

_____

_____

_____

_____

_____

_____

_____

_____

_____

_____

_____

_____

_____

practical
practice
praise
pray
prayer
preacher
precious
predict
prediction
preferred
prejudice
prepaid
prepare
present
preserving
president
pressure
pressurized
pretend
pretending
prettiest
pretty
prevent
previous
price
print
private
prize
prizes
problems
process
produce
program
project
promise
proof
prophet
protect
protection
proud
provide
provision
Psalms
public
published
puddle
pull
pumpkin
punished
puppy
purchase
pure
purity
purple
pursuit
push
pushing
put
puzzles

Qq
quack
quality
quantity
quarter
quarterback
queen
question
quick
quickly
quiet
quite
quizzes

Rr
rabbit
radio
raged
rainbow
raise
raisin
ran
rare
reached
reaching
read
reading
ready
realizes
really
reason
reasonable
reassure
rebuilt
recall
receipt
receive
received
recently
recognize
reconstruction
record
recount
recover
recreation
recycle
red
redrawn
references
refreshed
refreshing
refusal
refuse
refusing
regiment
regions
regular
rejoice
rejoicing
relate
relation

relief
relieve
remain
remainder
remarkable
remember
reminder
removed
repair
repay
repeat
repent
repentance
replied
reply
report
reporting
request
required
rescue
reserve
resignation
resigned
resources
respectful
responsible
rested
restore
restructured
resupply
resurrection
return
reusable
reverse
revise
revision
revival
revive
rewrote
rhyming
ribbon
rich
riddle
ride
rider
ridiculous
right
righteous
ringing
rink
rip
roadway
robin
rock
rocket
rode
roll
root
ropes
roses
rotation

rough
roughly
royal
royalty
rudely
rules
run
running
rupture
rush

Ss
sad
safe
safely
safety
said
sailboat
sailor
saints
salad
salary
salesclerk
salesman
salt
salvation
sandwich
sandwiches
sang
satisfactory
satisfy
Saturday
saucer
save
savings
Savior
saw
saying
says
scale
scarce
scare
scared
schedule
school
schools
science
scientist
scissors
score
scout
scramble
scraps
scratch
scratching
screen
scribe
Scripture
search
searching
seashore

seasonal
second
secret
section
security
see
seed
seen
selection
selfish
sense
sensible
sent
sentence
separate
September
sergeant
serious
servant
serve
service
services
session
set
settled
settlement
seven
seventeen
several
sewing
shadow
shall
shape
share
sharp
she
she's
sheet
shell
shelves
shelving
shepherd
shield
shine
shining
shoelace
shoes
shop
shopper
shortest
should
should've
shoulder
shouldn't
shovel
show
shower
shredded
shuttle
sick
side

_____
_____
_____
_____
_____
_____
_____
_____
_____
_____
_____
_____
_____
_____
_____
_____
_____
_____
_____
_____
_____
_____
_____
_____
_____
_____
_____
_____
_____
_____
_____
_____
_____
_____
_____
_____

sign	source	studied	tear	tigers
signal	south	studying	teeth	time
signaled	southern	stuff	telegram	tiny
signals	space	subject	telephone	tired
signature	spaghetti	submitting	telephoned	to
signatures	Spanish	substantial	televise	toast
signpost	sparkle	subtract	television	today
silver	speak	subtraction	televisions	toe
simple	special	such	tell	together
since	spell	suddenly	temple	told
sincere	spend	sugar	ten	tomatoes
sincerely	spider monkey	sugary	tendency	tomb
sing	Spirit	suggest	terrible	tomorrow
single	spiritual	suggestion	terrific	too
sink	splashed	suit	territory	took
sister	splinter	suitable	Testament	top
six	spoiled	suite	than	tossed
skate	spoke	summer	thank you	total
sketch artist	sponge	summertime	thankful	touchdown
skies	spot	sun	that	touched
skiing	spotless	sunburned	that's	toughest
skirts	spotlight	Sunday	the	tour
sky	sprained	sunflowers	their	toward
sleep	spray	superior	them	towel
sleepy	spread	supersonic	themselves	towels
slept	spring	supervisor	then	toys
slide	square	supply	there	track
slides	squares	suppose	there's	tractor
slow	squirrel	suppress	therefore	traffic
slowly	stacks	supreme	these	training
small	stalk	sure	they	transformation
smallest	standard	surely	they'll	transfusion
smile	star	surface	they're	transport
smother	start	surprise	they've	transportable
snack	station	surprised	thick	transportation
snakes	stayed	survey	thieves	transporting
snow	steady	survival	thing	travel agent
so	sticker	survivor	think	treasury
soar	still	swallow	thinking	treatment
soccer	stirring	sweater	third	trees
social	stitches	sweet	thirteen	tremendous
socks	stolen	swift	this	trial
soft	stood	swim	thorough	triangle
soldier	stop	swimming	those	tried
solution	stopped	swing	thought	triple
solve	storage	sympathy	thoughtful	troops
some	store	symptom	thoughtfulness	trouble
someone	storms	syrup	thousand	troublesome
someone's	story	systems	thread	troubling
someplace	straight		three	truck
something	straighten	**Tt**	threw	true
sometimes	strange	tabernacle	throat	truly
somewhere	strawberries	take	throne	trust
soon	straws	taken	through	trustworthy
sore	stream	talking	throw	truth
sorrow	stretch	tall	thrown	truthful
sorrowful	strict	tasting	thumb	try
sorry	strong	taught	thundercloud	Tuesday
soul	struck	teachable	Thursday	turn
sounded	structure	teacher	tickets	twelve
soupspoon	students	team	tickles	twenty-two

_____

_____

_____

_____

_____

_____

_____

_____

_____

_____

_____

_____

_____

_____

_____

_____

_____

_____

_____

_____

_____

_____

_____

twice
two
typist

Uu
umbrella
unbelief
uncertain
uncle's
under
understand
unexplained
unfair
unimportant
United States
universe
university
unknown
unless
unlikely
unloving
unreal
unspoken
unthinkable
until
untrue
unusual
up
upstairs
us
usable
used
usual

Vv
vacation
vain
valley
valuable
value
vault
vegetable
vegetables
verb
verbal
verbatim
verse
verses
version
very
video
video tape
view
village
vine
violin
visibility
visible
vision
visit

visitors
visors
visual
vital
vitality
vitamins
vivid
voice
volcano
volleyball
volumes
vowel
voyage

Ww
wages
wagon
waist
waiting
waitress
walk
walked
wall
wallpapered
wander
want
wanted
wants
warm
warmed
was
washer
washes
wasn't
wasps
waste
wastebasket
watch
watchman
water
watercolors
watermelons
waterproof
we
we'll
we're
we've
weak
wear
wearing
weary
weather
weave
Wednesday
week
weekend
weigh
weighed
weight
weird
welcome

well
went
were
weren't
what
what's
when
where
whether
which
while
whisper
whistle
white
who
who's
whoever
whole
wholesale
whose
why
will
win
wink
winner
winter
wire
wisdom
wise
wish
wishes
with
withdrew
without
wolves
woman
women
won't
wonderful
word
wore
worker
working
workmanship
world
worry
worse
worship
worst
would
would've
wouldn't
wound
wrecked
wring
wrinkle
write
writing
wrong
wrongly

Xx Yy Zz
yawned
yearn
years
yellow
yes
yesterday
yoke
you
you're
you've
young
your
yours
yourself
yourselves
youth
youthfulness
zebras
zero
zoo

_____

_____

_____

_____

_____

_____

_____

_____

_____

_____

_____

_____

_____

_____

_____

_____

_____

Personal Spelling Record

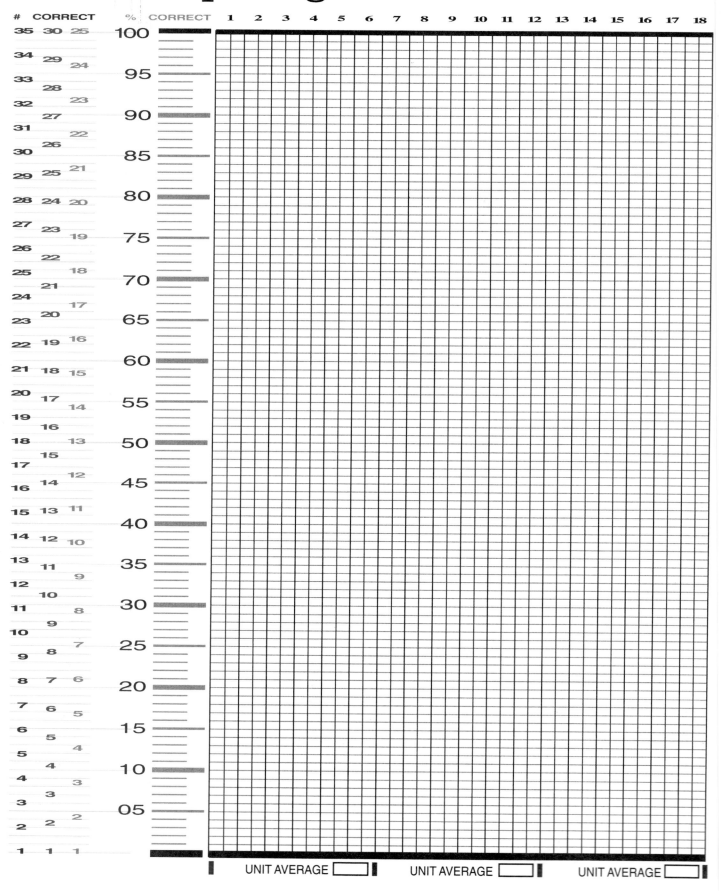